JAMESTOWN EDUCATION

Reading in the Content Areas

SOCIAL STUDIES

Based on the work of Walter Pauk

Mc Graw Hill Glencoe

New York, New York   Columbus, Ohio   Chicago, Illinois   Peoria, Illinois   Woodland Hills, California

JAMESTOWN 🚢 EDUCATION

Readability

Tab 1: Levels D–F
Tab 2: Levels G–I
Tab 3: Levels J–K
Tab 4: Levels L–L+

Cover photo: © Bill Frymire/Masterfile

Glencoe

The *McGraw·Hill* Companies

ISBN: 0-07-861708-1

Send all queries to:
Glencoe/McGraw-Hill
8787 Orion Place
Columbus, OH 43240-4027

7 8 9 10 079 08 07 06

Contents

To the Student

To succeed in the courses you take, one of the most important skills you can have is good reading ability. Different courses require different types of reading. If material is easy for you or if you have studied it before, you may read quickly. If the material is new or difficult, you may read slowly. In fact, you need to read the material several times. You can use the reading skills featured in this book in all your courses.

The passages in the book are readings in social studies. Within this subject area are several subcategories, including history, geography, and anthropology.

This book does not require you to master many new facts. Instead, its purpose is to show you *how to read social studies information.* You will learn techniques that textbook writers use to organize material. You will see how new information can be added to what you already know. And you will learn about the six skills that can help you read just about anything.

The Six Types of Questions

In this book, the basic skills necessary for reading factual material are taught through the use of the following six types of questions: main idea, subject matter, supporting details, conclusion, clarifying devices, and vocabulary in context.

Main Idea. Whenever you read, it is a good idea to ask yourself, What point is the writer trying to make? Once you ask this question, your mind will be looking for an answer, and chances are that you will find one. But if you don't focus in this way, all things seem equal. Nothing stands out.

Try to find the main idea in the following passage by asking yourself, What point is the writer trying to make?

> A horseshoe means good luck. This is true in every country. The good luck comes partly because the shoe is made of iron and partly because its shape is like a crescent moon. It is very good luck to find a horseshoe by the side of the road. It is extra good luck if the shoe was thrown from the right rear leg of a gray mare. Horseshoes are usually hung over the outside doorways of houses.

What is the main idea? Here's a good answer: Horseshoes mean good luck. This passage is easy to figure out because the first sentence is an excellent topic sentence.

The next example does not have a topic sentence. Nevertheless, you can still answer the question, What point is the writer trying to make? This time, think about the passage and come up with your own answer.

Most people traveled the Oregon Trail by covered wagon. Inside the wagon were all their possessions. Women and children usually rode and slept in there. Wagons had canvas tops. These were soaked in oil, which made them rainproof. Usually oxen pulled the wagons. People brought these animals along to plow their new farms. Often the oxen had to be pushed up mountain passes. When wagons got stuck in the mud, people would lighten the wagons by throwing out possessions. If there was no bridge, the oxen had to drag the wagons across the water.

This passage may have required a bit more thought, for the correct answer is a summary type answer. Compare your answer with the following main idea statement: Travel along the Oregon Trail was often difficult.

Subject Matter. This question looks easy. But don't think it isn't important. The subject matter question can help you with the most important reading and learning skill of all: concentration. With it, you comprehend and learn. Without it, you fail.

Here is the secret for concentrating: After reading a few lines of a passage, ask yourself, What is the subject matter of this passage? Instantly, you will be thinking about the passage. You will be concentrating. If you don't ask this question, your eyes may move across the print, yet your mind may be thinking of other things.

By asking this question as you read each passage in this book, you will master the skill so well that it will carry over to everything you read.

Let's see how this method works. Here is a short passage.

Sometimes people say "going to Timbuktu" when they are traveling to a faraway, isolated place. Did you know that there really is a place called Timbuktu? For centuries it was a very important city in Africa.

On finishing the first sentence, your thought should have been something like this: *Ah, a passage on Timbuktu. Maybe I can learn something about this faraway place.* If it was, your head was in the right place. By focusing right away on the subject matter, you will be concentrating, you will be looking for something, and—best of all—you will be understanding, learning, and remembering.

Supporting Details. In common usage, the word *detail* has taken on the meaning of "something relatively unimportant." But details are important. Details are the plaster, board, and brick of a building, while main ideas are the large strong steel or wooden beams. A solid, well-written passage must contain both.

The bulk of a factual passage is made up of details that support the main idea. The main idea is often buried among the details. You have to dig to distinguish between the main idea and the details. Here are some characteristics that can help you see the difference between supporting details and main ideas.

First, supporting details come in various forms. They can be examples, explanations, descriptions, definitions, comparisons, contrasts, exceptions, analogies, similes, and metaphors.

Second, these various kinds of details support the main idea. The words themselves—*supporting details*—spell out their job. When you have trouble finding the main idea, take a passage apart sentence by sentence. Ask yourself, Does this sentence support something, or is this the idea being supported? You must not only separate the main idea from the details, you must also see how they help one another. The main idea can often be expressed in a sentence. But a sentence cannot tell a complete story. The writer must use additional sentences to give a full picture.

The following passage shows how important details are for providing a full picture of what the writer had in mind.

> The Amazon is the mightiest river for this reason. It discharges the greatest amount of water. More water flows out to sea from the Amazon than from the Nile, Mississippi, and Yangtze Rivers combined. That's a lot of fresh water! The force of its current is great too. The current can be seen 200 miles out in the sea. Here's a story to show the Amazon's amazing current. A sailing ship was far out of sight of Brazil. It ran out of drinking water. A passing ship drew alongside. The captain of the first ship asked for water. The captain of the second ship said, "Just dip your buckets over the side."

The main idea is in the first two sentences. After stating the main idea, the writer gives several examples showing why it is true. The examples are supporting details.

Conclusion. As a reader moves through a passage, grasping the main idea and the supporting details, it is natural for him or her to begin to guess an ending or a conclusion. Some passages contain conclusions; others do not. It depends on the writer's purpose. For example, some passages simply describe a process—how something is done. It is not always necessary to draw a conclusion from such a passage.

In some passages with conclusions, the writer states the conclusion. But in most passages in this book, the conclusion is merely implied. That is, the writer seems to have come to a conclusion but has not stated it. It is up to you to draw that conclusion.

In the following passage, the writer implies a conclusion but does not state it.

> The hamburg steak was brought to America in the nineteenth century by German immigrants. Louis Lassen, a cook in New Haven, Connecticut, modified the hamburg steak by sandwiching it between two pieces of bread. But the true American hamburger came into existence in St. Louis at the Louisiana Purchase Exposition in 1904. A harried cook at the fair quickly slapped broiled beef patties between buns and served them to a demanding crowd, which gulped them down joyously.

From this passage, we can draw the conclusion that the original hamburger was somewhat of an accident.

Sometimes a writer will ask you to draw a conclusion by applying what you have learned to a new situation, as in the following passage.

> In July 1918 the entire family of Czar Nicholas II of Russia was assassinated by Bolshevik revolutionaries in Siberia. Almost immediately, rumors began that the youngest daughter, 17-year-old Anastasia, had been spared, and pretenders began to proliferate. One woman, Anna Anderson, claimed to be Anastasia until her death in 1948. DNA testing has laid Anderson's story to rest. She was proven to be a fraud when the remains of all of Nicholas's children were found at the assassination site and identified.

If you were asked what this passage suggests about the value of DNA testing, you would have to generalize beyond the passage. You might say you can draw the conclusion that there will be fewer false identity claims because of DNA testing.

Looking for a conclusion puts you in the shoes of a detective. While reading, you have to think, Where is the writer leading me? What conclusion will I be able to draw? And, like a detective, you must try to guess the conclusion, changing the guess as you get more and more information.

Clarifying Devices. Clarifying devices are words, phrases, and techniques that a writer uses to make main ideas and supporting details clear and interesting. By knowing some of these clarifying and controlling devices, you will be better able to recognize them in the passages you read. By recognizing them, you will be able to read with greater comprehension and speed.

Transitional or Signal Words. The largest single group of clarifying devices, and the most widely used, is transitional or signal words. Here are some signal words that you see all the time: *first, second, next, last,* and *finally.* A writer uses such words to keep ideas, steps in a process, or lists in order. Other transitional words include *however, in brief, in conclusion, above all, therefore, since, because,* and *consequently.*

When you see transitional words, consider what they mean. A transitional word like *or* tells you that another option, or choice, is coming. Words like *but* and *however* signal that a contrast, or change in point of view, will follow.

Organizational Patterns. Organizational patterns are also clarifying devices. One such pattern is the chronological pattern, in which events unfold in the order of time: one thing happens first, then another, and so on. A time pattern orders events. The incident may take place in five minutes or over a period of hundreds of years.

There are other organizational patterns as well. Writers may use spatial descriptions to tell what things look like. They may use lists of examples to make their point. In social studies writing, they may use data that has been collected by specialists. Seeing the organizational pattern will help you read the material more easily.

Textual Devices. Textbook writers often use patterns or particular text styles to make their ideas clear. Bulleted lists, subheads, and boldfaced or italicized words help to highlight important ideas in the text. Concepts shown in charts or diagrams may be easier to understand than concepts explained in words alone.

Literal Versus Figurative Language. Sometimes words do not mean what they seem to mean on first reading. For example, a writer may say, "The tragedy shattered the hero of the story." You may know *shattered* means "breaking into pieces." The word is often applied to breakable objects, but here it is applied to a person's feelings. Being alert to special meanings can help you appreciate the writer's meaning.

Two literary devices that writers use to present ideas in interesting ways are similes (SIM-a-leez) and metaphors (MET-a-forz). Both are used to make comparisons that add color and power to ideas. A simile uses the word *like* or *as.* Here's an example of a simile: She has a mind like a computer. Here, a person's mind is compared to a computer. A metaphor makes a direct comparison: Her mind is a computer.

Vocabulary in Context. How accurately do you use words you already know? Do you know that *exotic* means "a thing or a person from a foreign country"? Exotic costumes are costumes from foreign countries. *Exotic* has been used incorrectly so often and for so long that it has developed a second meaning. Many people use *exotic* to mean "strikingly unusual in color or design."

Many people think that the words *imply* and *infer* mean the same thing. They do not. A writer may imply, or suggest, something. The reader then infers what the writer implied. In other words, to imply is to "suggest an idea." To infer is to "take meaning out" or to "draw a conclusion."

It is easy to see what would happen to a passage if a reader skipped a word or two that he or she did not know and imposed fuzzy meanings on a few others. The result would inevitably be a gross misunderstanding of the writer's message. You will become a better reader if you learn the exact meanings and the various shades of meaning of the words that are already familiar to you.

In this book, you should be able to figure out the meanings of many words from their context—that is, from the words and phrases around them. If this method does not work for you, however, you may consult a dictionary.

Answering the Main Idea Question

The main idea questions in this book are not the usual multiple-choice variety that asks you to select the one correct statement. Rather, you are given three statements and are asked to select the statement that expresses the main idea of the passage, the statement that is too narrow, and the statement that is too broad. You have to work hard to identify all three statements correctly. This new type of question teaches you to recognize the differences between statements that, at first, seem almost equal.

To help you handle these questions, let's go behind the scenes to see how the main idea questions in this book were constructed. The true main idea statement was always written first. It had to be neat and succinct. The main idea tells who or what is the subject of the passage. The main idea statement also tells what the subject is doing or what the subject is like. Next, keeping the main idea statement in mind, the other two statements were written. They are variations of the main idea statement. The "too narrow" statement had to express only part of the main idea. The "too broad" statement had to be very general in scope.

Read the passage below. Then, to learn how to answer the main idea questions, follow the instructions in the box. The answer to each part of the question has been filled in for you. The score for each answer has also been marked.

The Children's Crusade

The Fifth Crusade will live in history. It is truly an unforgettable tragedy. This crusade was better known as the Children's Crusade. It took place in 1212 and burned itself into the hearts, minds, memories, and imaginations of almost all the people in Europe. People felt bad about it for many years. The reason for the long lingering remorse might be that they did not undestand why the parents had let their children go. The Holy Land was a thousand miles away. Didn't the parents foresee the life-and-death hardships? Did they think some magic carpet would whisk their children to the Holy Land?

This crusade was made up of young boys and girls. Many of the children were less than 12 years old. There were two armies of children. One army was from France; the other was from Germany. Neither reached the Holy Land. Almost no children ever returned to their homes.

What happened to most of the children? Some died of hunger. Many died of cold weather. Fatigue took its toll, as did disease. It is a long march to the Mediterranean Sea. Some marchers did reach the sea, but the sea was stormy. Most children were drowned in overloaded ships. Some reached the shore of Africa, but then they were captured and sold as slaves.

	Answer	Score
Mark the *main idea*	M	15
Mark the statement that is *too broad*	B	5
Mark the statement that is *too narrow*	N	5

a. The Children's Crusade led to the tragic death of many children.   M   15

[This statement gathers all the important points. It gives a correct picture of the main idea in a brief way: (1) Children's Crusade, (2) many children, and (3) tragic deaths.]

b. Many children in the Crusade were less than 12 years old.   N   5

[This statement is correct, but it is too narrow. Only part of the main idea is included. Mention of the children's deaths is left out.]

c. The death of young boys and girls is sad and unforgettable.   B   5

[This statement is too broad. It mentions children's deaths, but it does not focus on the specific deaths that are the subject of the passage: those of the children in the Children's Crusade.]

Getting the Most Out of This Book

The following steps could be called "tricks of the trade" or "rules for learning." It doesn't matter what they are called. What does matter is that they work.

Think about the title. A famous language expert proposes the following "trick" to use when reading. "The first thing to do is to read the title. Then spend a few moments thinking about it."

Writers spend much time thinking up good titles. They try to pack a lot of meaning into them. It makes sense for you to spend a few seconds trying to dig out some meaning. These moments of thought will give you a head start on a passage. Thinking about the title can help you in another way too. It helps you concentrate on a passage before you begin reading. Why does this happen? Thinking about the title fills your head with thoughts about the passage. There's no room for anything else to get in to break your concentration.

The Dot Step. Here is a method that will speed up your reading. It also builds comprehension at the same time.

Spend a few moments with the title. Then read quickly through the passage. Next, without looking back, answer the six questions by placing a dot in the box next to each answer of your choice. The dots will be your "unofficial" answers. For the main idea question (question 1), place your dot in the box next to the statement that you think is the main idea.

The dot system helps by making you think hard on your first fast reading. The practice you gain by trying to grasp and remember ideas makes you a stronger reader.

The Checkmark Step. First, answer the main idea question. Follow the steps that are given above each set of statements for this question. Use a capital letter to mark your final answer to each part of the main idea question.

You have answered the other five questions with a dot. Now read the passage once more carefully. This time, mark your final answer to each question by placing a checkmark (√) in the box next to the answer of your choice. The answers with the checkmarks are the ones that will count toward your score.

The Diagnostic Chart. Now move your final answers to the Diagnostic Chart for the passage. These charts start on page 155.

Use the row of boxes beside Passage 1 for the answers to the first passage. Use the row of boxes beside Passage 2 for the answers to the second passage, and so on. Write the letter of your answer to the left of the dotted line in each block.

Correct your answers using the Answer Keys on pages 152–154. When scoring your answers, do not use an *x* for incorrect or a *c* for correct. Instead, use this method: If your choice is incorrect, write the letter of the correct answer to the right of the dotted line in the block.

Thus, the row of answers for each passage will show your incorrect answers. And it will also show the correct answers.

Your Total Comprehension Score. Go back to the passage. If you answered a question incorrectly, draw a line under the correct choice on the question page. Then write your score for each question on the line provided. Add the scores to get your total comprehension score. Enter that score in the Total Score box.

Graphing Your Progress. After finding your total comprehension score, turn to the Progress Graphs (pages 158–160). Write your score in the box for the passage. Then put an *x* along the line above the box to show your total comprehension score. Join the *x*'s as you go. This will plot a line showing your progress.

Taking Corrective Action. Your incorrect answers give you a way to teach yourself how to read better. Take the time to study these answers.

Go back to the questions. For each question you answered wrong, read the correct answer (the one you have underlined) several times. With the correct answer in mind, go back to the passage itself. Read to see why the given answer is better. Try to see where you made your mistake and why you chose an incorrect answer.

The Steps in a Nutshell

Here's a quick review of the steps to follow. Following these steps is the way to get the most out of this book. Be sure you have read and understood everything in this To the Student section before you begin reading the passages.

1. **Think about the title of the passage.** Try to get all the meaning the writer put into it.
2. **Read the passage quickly.**
3. **Answer the questions, using the dot system.** Use dots to mark your unofficial answers. Don't look back at the passage.
4. **Read the passage again—carefully.**
5. **Mark your final answers.** Put a checkmark (√) in the box to note your final answer. Use capital letters for each part of the main idea question.
6. **Mark your answers on the diagnostic chart.** Record your final answers on the diagnostic chart for the passage. Write your answers to the left of the dotted line in the answer blocks for the passage.
7. **Correct your answers.** Use the answer keys on pages 152–154. If an answer is not correct, write the correct answer on the right side of the block, beside your incorrect answer. Then go back to the question page. Place a line under the correct answer.
8. **Find your total comprehension score.** Find this by adding up the points you earned for each question. Enter the total in the box marked Total Score.
9. **Graph your progress.** Enter and plot your score on the progress graph for that passage.
10. **Take corrective action.** Read your wrong answers. Read the passage once more. Try to figure out why you were wrong.

To the Teacher

The Reading Passages

Each of the 75 passages included in this book is related to social studies. Within this subject area are several subcategories, for example, history, geography, and anthropology.

Each passage had to meet the following two criteria: high interest level and appropriate readability level. The high interest level was assured by choosing passages of mature content that would appeal to a wide range of readers.

The readability level of each passage was computed by applying Dr. Edward B. Fry's *Formula for Estimating Readability*. The passages within the book are arranged according to reading levels. *Reading in the Content Areas: Social Studies* contains 75 passages that range from reading level 4 to reading level 12+. The passages are organized into four ranges of reading levels, as indicated by color tabs: The first passages range from reading level 4 to reading level 6. The next passages range from reading level 7 to reading level 9. The third group of passages ranges from reading level 10 to reading level 11. The final passages range from reading level 12 to reading level 12+.

The Six Questions

This book is organized around six essential questions. The most important of these is the main idea question, which is actually a set of three statements. Students must first choose and label the statement that expresses the main idea of the passage; then they must label each of the other statements as either too narrow or too broad to be the main idea.

In addition to the main idea question, there are five other questions. These questions are within the framework of the following five categories: subject matter, supporting details, conclusion, clarifying devices, and vocabulary in context.

By repeated practice with answering the questions within these six categories, students will develop an active searching attitude about what they read. These six types of questions will help them become aware of what they are reading at the time they are actually seeing the words and phrases on a page. This thinking-while-reading sets the stage for higher comprehension and better retention.

The Diagnostic Chart

The Diagnostic Chart provides the most dignified form of guidance yet devised. With this chart, no one has to point out a student's weaknesses. The chart does that automatically, yielding the information directly and personally to the student, making self-teaching possible. The organization of the questions and the format for marking answers on the chart are what make it work so well.

The six questions for each passage are always in the same order. For example, the question designed to teach the skill of drawing conclusions is always the fourth question, and the main idea question is always first. Keeping the questions in order sets the stage for the smooth working of the chart.

The chart works automatically when students write the letter of their answer choices for each passage in the spaces provided. Even after completing only one passage, the chart will reveal the types of questions answered correctly, as well as the types answered incorrectly. As the answers for more passages are recorded, the chart will show the types of questions that are missed consistently. A pattern can be seen after three or more passages have been completed. For example, if a student answers question 4 (drawing conclusions) incorrectly for three out of four passages, the student's weakness in this area shows up automatically.

Once a weakness is revealed, have your students take the following steps: First, turn to the instructional pages in the beginning of the book and study the section in which the topic is discussed. Second, go back and reread the questions that were missed in that particular category. Then, with the correct answer to a question in mind, read the entire passage again, trying to see how the writer developed the answer to the question. Do this for each question that was missed. Third, when reading future passages, make an extra effort to correctly answer the questions in that particular category. Fourth, if the difficulty continues, arrange to see your teacher.

Reading in the Content Areas
SOCIAL STUDIES

1 History: What It Is, What It Means

Do you know what history is? Here is one answer. It is everything humans have done and thought. Here is a more specific answer. History is the story of events. It is the story of nations and persons. How people began writing is part of history. So is the Hundred Years' War. So is the first airplane flight. So is last year's election.

How do we know about the past? There are many sources. Some are oral. Some are visual or written. We can learn of the past from one person's memory. We can learn from stories handed down through generations. We can see the past in a piece of Stone Age flint. We see it in old paintings and photos. We read about the past in old records. They may be ships' logs or church records. They may be diaries of pioneers. They may be journals of presidents. Each fact and story is interesting. Each is important. Each is part of history.

It is impossible to record everything about an event or person. Facts must be carefully chosen to tell what happened. Questions have to be asked. Answers must be found. Different accounts of a single event need to be put together.

This is the job of historians. They try to come up with an <u>accurate</u> story. They look carefully at what they find. Then they put the past together again. Historians search for causes of events. They also look for history's effects. Sometimes they do not know how or why something happened. Then they come up with theories. These theories are based on the facts. They may help explain certain events.

When the facts are put together, a story of events and nations comes forth. The story of humans can be told.

Main Idea 1

	Answer	Score
Mark the *main idea*	M	15
Mark the statement that is *too broad*	B	5
Mark the statement that is *too narrow*	N	5

a. History is the Hundred Years' War and the first airplane flight. ☐ _____

b. To understand history, facts must be studied and analyzed. ☐ _____

c. History is all about the past. ☐ _____

Subject Matter   **2**   Another good title for this passage is
- ☐ a. A History of the World.
- ☐ b. The Story of Nations.
- ☐ c. How to Become a Historian.
- ☐ d. Making Sense of History.   _____

Supporting Details   **3**   Which of the following is an example of a visual history source?
- ☐ a. an old photograph
- ☐ b. a diary
- ☐ c. a person's memory
- ☐ d. stories   _____

Conclusion   **4**   To be a good historian, a person must **not**
- ☐ a. want to know about the past.
- ☐ b. be in a hurry.
- ☐ c. be able to analyze information.
- ☐ d. read a lot.   _____

Clarifying Devices   **5**   The question in the second paragraph tells the reader that the sentences that follow will
- ☐ a. list some sources of historical information.
- ☐ b. tell why there is no information about the past.
- ☐ c. tell why history confuses the writer.
- ☐ d. give reasons why history is important.   _____

Vocabulary in Context   **6**   The word <u>accurate</u> means
- ☐ a. mistaken.
- ☐ b. agreeable.
- ☐ c. believable.
- ☐ d. correct.   _____

Add your scores for questions 1–6. Enter the total here and on the graph on page 158.   **Total Score**   _____

2 The Roman Army

The Roman Empire was a great power in ancient times. But the first Roman army was made up of ordinary citizens. Young men did the fighting. Older men cleaned weapons and defended their cities. They served only in crisis or war. Then the time came when Rome needed well-trained men. A new army of full-time, paid soldiers was created. The men were called legionaries. Legionaries stayed in the army for 20 years. They trained, fought, and built roads and bridges. The legionaries served in groups called legions. Each legion was made up of about 6,000 men. At the height of the Roman Empire, around 27 B.C., 28 legions served the empire.

Legionaries carried their weapons, clothes, tents, food, and cooking pots. They marched about 21 miles a day. When they came to a river, they built a bridge. Each night they set up camp. They built earth walls to protect the camp from attack. They also built roads so the army could march between towns and camps. About 50,000 miles of highways were built. They connected all parts of the Roman Empire. (Some parts of these roads still exist today.)

Sometimes the Roman army attacked towns. A town might have walls made of thick stone. Its gate would be heavy and wooden. The town's soldiers defended the town, hurling spears and shooting arrows from the top of the walls. The attacking Roman soldiers used a movable tower. They pushed the tower toward the enemy's walls. They lowered a drawbridge from the tower to the top of the wall. Then the Roman soldiers swarmed across the drawbridge to capture the town.

At their peak, no one equaled the Romans, their army, or their empire. They had no rivals.

Main Idea	1		
		Answer	**Score**
	Mark the *main idea*	M	15
	Mark the statement that is *too broad*	B	5
	Mark the statement that is *too narrow*	N	5
	a. The Romans had a very large empire.	☐	_____
	b. The Roman army was an important part of the Roman Empire.	☐	_____
	c. The Roman legions sometimes attacked heavily defended towns.	☐	_____

Subject Matter 2 This passage is mostly about
☐ a. what the Roman legions did.
☐ b. who trained Roman soldiers.
☐ c. why Roman roads survive to this day.
☐ d. the Roman army before the legions
were formed. _____

Supporting 3 The legionaries carried
Details ☐ a. road maps.
☐ b. a drawbridge.
☐ c. their tents.
☐ d. movable towers. _____

Conclusion 4 Which adjective best describes the Roman army?
☐ a. vicious
☐ b. well-trained
☐ c. weak
☐ d. small _____

Clarifying 5 The date 27 B.C. in the first paragraph refers to
Devices ☐ a. the first year that Rome had a full-time army.
☐ b. the year that 50,000 miles of roads were built.
☐ c. the year the Roman army invented
movable towers.
☐ d. the time when the Roman Empire was
largest and most powerful. _____

Vocabulary 6 In this passage, the word <u>rivals</u> means
in Context ☐ a. equals.
☐ b. crimes.
☐ c. leaders.
☐ d. friends. _____

Add your scores for questions 1–6. Enter the total here **Total**
and on the graph on page 158. **Score** _____

3 What Is Geography?

Geography is an old area of study. It goes back to early Greece. The Greeks wrote about the natural world. They noted where things were on the earth. The word *geography* comes from the Greeks. It means "earth description."

Geographers today describe the earth. They describe the size of land masses. They study the seas. They collect data on climates. They watch plant and animal life. They also look for connections. Connections mean a lot to them. In fact, connections are <u>foremost</u> in their studies. They try to connect people with the earth.

Geographers look at people and the earth in four ways. First, they think about location. Location means where people and places are. Location tells exactly where something is. It also tells if something is near or far.

Second, they study relationships. They see how places affect people's lives. They figure out why people and things are where they are.

Third, they look at movement. They note how goods and people go from place to place.

Finally, they look at regions. These are areas with names. Regions are named for governments. They are named for languages. They may be named for religious groups. They are sometimes named for ethnic groups. They may also be named for landforms or climate.

Maps and globes are the geographer's tools. Census counts and land surveys are tools too. So are photos and satellites. They tell about remote places.

Geographers study many things. They study climate. They examine land. They look at population. They study economics. They note how one thing affects another. They try to see how people and the earth fit together.

Main Idea	1		
		Answer	**Score**
Mark the *main idea*		M	15
Mark the statement that is *too broad*		B	5
Mark the statement that is *too narrow*		N	5

a. Geographers use tools such as maps and globes. ☐ _____

b. Geography is interesting. ☐ _____

c. Geography is the study of connections between people and the earth. ☐ _____

Subject Matter 2 This passage explains that geography is
- ☐ a. the study of many aspects of the earth.
- ☐ b. the study of photography and satellites.
- ☐ c. a religious group.
- ☐ d. the study of ancient Greece. _____

Supporting Details 3 The passage discusses how many ways to look at people and the earth?
- ☐ a. two
- ☐ b. four
- ☐ c. six
- ☐ d. ten _____

Conclusion 4 For a geographer, the phrase "Spanish-speaking" might identify a
- ☐ a. movement.
- ☐ b. region.
- ☐ c. satellite.
- ☐ d. relationship. _____

Clarifying Devices 5 In the first paragraph, the phrase "earth description" is used as
- ☐ a. a simile.
- ☐ b. a definition.
- ☐ c. a name for the early Greeks.
- ☐ d. one of several ways of looking at the earth. _____

Vocabulary in Context 6 The word <u>foremost</u> means
- ☐ a. debated.
- ☐ b. forgotten.
- ☐ c. first.
- ☐ d. fourth. _____

Add your scores for questions 1–6. Enter the total here and on the graph on page 158. **Total Score** _____

4 The Caves of Lascaux

Imagine looking for your lost dog. You step into a cave. But instead of the dog, you find beautiful cave paintings. You see paintings of horses, deer, and bison. They are drawn in black, brown, red, and yellow. Your first question would probably be "Who did this?"

This is what happened to four French boys in 1940. They found the Lascaux (la skō′) caves. The paintings the boys discovered in those caves are 17,000 years old. They were drawn by the prehistoric people called Cro-Magnons.

Cro-Magnons looked much like people of today. They used tools, such as fishing nets, that look familiar too. But their art was <u>extraordinary</u>. The main cave at Lascaux is called the Great Hall of Bulls. It has a picture of bulls and horses in many colors. The largest animal is 18 feet long. There are smaller animals too. They include bison, stags, and a bear. There is also an odd, spotted, two-horned animal.

To the left of the main cave are the most famous paintings. These are drawings of multicolored animals. One painting is called Little Horses. On the ceiling are horses and cows. The most unusual sight may be in the Shaft of the Dead Man. Here is a rhinoceros, a carefully drawn dead man, a wounded bison, and a bird.

Why did Cro-Magnon artists do these beautiful drawings on cave walls? Did the drawings call upon some magical power? Did the Cro-Magnon people hope that the drawings would bring luck? There is one thing the paintings seem to tell us. The Cro-Magnons had a sense of wonder about the world. They looked at beauty and they understood it.

Main Idea 1

	Answer	Score
Mark the *main idea*	M	15
Mark the statement that is *too broad*	B	5
Mark the statement that is *too narrow*	N	5

a. Cave paintings are beautiful.	☐	____
b. The caves of Lascaux hold colorful prehistoric paintings.	☐	____
c. Drawings of horses are on the walls of the Lascaux caves.	☐	____

Score 15 points for each correct answer.   **Score**

Subject Matter **2** The main topic of this passage is
- ☐ a. the lives of Cro-Magnon people.
- ☐ b. animals of prehistoric times.
- ☐ c. what the cave paintings of Lascaux looked like.
- ☐ d. the boys who discovered the paintings.   _____

Supporting Details **3** Most of the drawings in the caves are of
- ☐ a. several types of animals.
- ☐ b. horses.
- ☐ c. dead people.
- ☐ d. teenage boys.   _____

Conclusion **4** The writer would like you to conclude that
- ☐ a. anyone can find cave art.
- ☐ b. the cave paintings of Lascaux are remarkable.
- ☐ c. the Cro-Magnon people are a mystery.
- ☐ d. the Cro-Magnon people were magicians.   _____

Clarifying Devices **5** The writer uses the word *you* in the first paragraph to
- ☐ a. give the reader good directions to find the caves.
- ☐ b. pull the reader into the story.
- ☐ c. compare present-day readers with Cro-Magnon people.
- ☐ d. make it clear that this is a true story.   _____

Vocabulary in Context **6** The word extraordinary means
- ☐ a. about animals.
- ☐ b. familiar.
- ☐ c. colorful.
- ☐ d. very unusual.   _____

Add your scores for questions 1–6. Enter the total here and on the graph on page 158.   **Total Score**   _____

9

5 A Separation of Powers

The U.S. Constitution was written in 1787. The states finally worked out their differences and <u>ratified</u> the Constitution in 1788.

James Madison, the author of the Constitution, wanted a strong government with three branches. These three branches balance each other's power.

The *executive branch* is the office of the president. (It also includes his or her cabinet.) This branch enforces federal laws. It appoints federal officials. It deals with foreign countries. The president is commander of the armed forces.

The *judicial branch* includes the Supreme Court. It also includes the lower Federal Courts. It decides cases of law.

The *legislative branch* makes laws. It also amends and repeals laws and collects taxes. One part of this branch is the Senate. It has 100 members. Each state has two senators. The other part is the House of Representatives. It has 435 members. Each state sends a number of representatives based on its population.

How many representatives would there be? Madison said the number should reflect how many people live in a state. New Jersey had few people. These people did not agree. They said each state should have the same number of representatives. The people of Connecticut wanted a compromise. They said the law-making branch should have two parts. In one part, each state would have the same number of members. In the other part, the number of members from a state would vary. Large states would have more members. Small states would have fewer.

Main Idea	1	Answer	Score
	Mark the *main idea*	M	15
	Mark the statement that is *too broad*	B	5
	Mark the statement that is *too narrow*	N	5

a. The U.S. Constitution provides for three branches of government. ☐ _____

b. The United States has a Constitution. ☐ _____

c. The Senate has 100 members. ☐ _____

Score 15 points for each correct answer.   **Score**

Subject Matter   **2**   Another good title for this passage is
    ☐ a. A Battle Between the States.
    ☐ b. James Madison, American Hero.
    ☐ c. Three Branches Equals One Government.
    ☐ d. More than 200 Years Ago.   _____

Supporting   **3**   The legislative branch deals mainly with
Details
    ☐ a. the armed forces.
    ☐ b. the making of laws.
    ☐ c. the courts.
    ☐ d. foreign policy.   _____

Conclusion   **4**   Which statement best describes the final
Constitution?
    ☐ a. It uses only James Madison's ideas.
    ☐ b. It is a compromise between the states.
    ☐ c. It does not represent small states.
    ☐ d. It gives most of the power to the president.   _____

Clarifying   **5**   In this passage, the words *legislative branch* are in
Devices   italic type as an example of
    ☐ a. a main title.
    ☐ b. a quotation.
    ☐ c. an author's byline.
    ☐ d. an important term.   _____

Vocabulary   **6**   The word ratified in this passage means
in Context
    ☐ a. formally and officially approved.
    ☐ b. raised another's child as one's own.
    ☐ c. chosen for use in a classroom.
    ☐ d. admired greatly.   _____

Add your scores for questions 1–6. Enter the total here   **Total**
and on the graph on page 158.   **Score**   _____

6 Capital of the Inca Empire

Cuzco was the capital city of the Inca Empire in South America. The empire began in the 1300s. It ended suddenly in 1532. At its peak, the empire had 12 million people. Peru, Ecuador, and parts of Chile, Bolivia, and Argentina made up the empire. The city of Cuzco was the <u>hub</u>. Inca roads spread from the city like spokes on a wheel. The roads went to the four corners of the empire. The roads brought the empire's treasure of silver and gold into Cuzco.

Cuzco had palaces, temples, and government buildings. The most important buildings were made from fine stonework. Inca architects planned these buildings. First they made clay models. Then workers dug huge blocks of limestone and granite from the ground. Next skilled stonemasons cut and fit the blocks together. The stonemasons shaped each stone. They used stone hammers and bronze chisels. Thousands of workers hauled the blocks into place. Stone blocks weighed as much as 20 tons. The workers moved the blocks with ropes and wooden rollers. To get heavy stones to the top of high walls, workers dragged them up earth ramps. Incas sanded and polished the stone blocks. The blocks fit together perfectly. There were no gaps or spaces. Only a line showed where the blocks were joined.

The Spaniards destroyed much of Cuzco in 1533. They built a new Spanish city on top of the old one. Some of their buildings have the old Inca buildings as their foundations. Sometimes they used the Incas' stones to build new buildings. They used Inca gold and silver to decorate their churches. The empire is gone now, but Incan skill and wealth remain.

Main Idea	1		Answer	Score
	Mark the *main idea*		M	15
	Mark the statement that is *too broad*		B	5
	Mark the statement that is *too narrow*		N	5

a. Cuzco was a city in the Inca Empire. ☐ _____

b. The Spaniards decorated their churches with Inca gold. ☐ _____

c. The buildings of Cuzco were built with skill and wealth. ☐ _____

Score 15 points for each correct answer.   **Score**

Subject Matter   2   This passage is mainly about
- [ ] a. the Spanish destruction of Cuzco.
- [ ] b. the skill of Inca builders.
- [ ] c. the location of the Inca Empire.
- [ ] d. the modern city of Cuzco.   _____

Supporting Details   3   Buildings in the Inca city of Cuzco were
- [ ] a. made of clay.
- [ ] b. homes for 12 million people.
- [ ] c. made of fine stonework.
- [ ] d. built quickly.   _____

Conclusion   4   In the last paragraph, the phrase "Incan skill and wealth remain" means
- [ ] a. Incas still live and work in Cuzco.
- [ ] b. Spaniards love the Incan treasures.
- [ ] c. buildings and gold are preserved in museums.
- [ ] d. Inca stone blocks and gold still exist in Cuzco.   _____

Clarifying Devices   5   The Incan roads are compared to
- [ ] a. the spokes of a wheel.
- [ ] b. stone hammers and bronze chisels.
- [ ] c. four corners of an empire.
- [ ] d. the treasures of gold and silver.   _____

Vocabulary in Context   6   In this passage, the word <u>hub</u> means the
- [ ] a. best.
- [ ] b. center of importance.
- [ ] c. noisy part of the empire.
- [ ] d. center of a wheel.   _____

Add your scores for questions 1–6. Enter the total here and on the graph on page 158.   **Total Score**   _____

7 What Is Social Studies?

A 1987 <u>survey</u> was given to 5,000 high school seniors. It showed that they did not know geography. Students in Boston were questioned. One-third of them could not name six New England states. Students in Baltimore were questioned. Half could not shade in the United States on a map. Here is what another survey showed. Students did not know history. Most did not know the dates of the Civil War. Many did not know World War II leaders.

Someone else asked this question. What did students think of social studies? Their answer: Social studies was not important. They said it was the least important of their studies.

What is social studies? It is the study of individuals. It is the study of groups. It is the study of societies. Social studies covers many fields. You have read about history and geography. These are part of social studies. It covers many other areas as well. Let's say you study the way people live together in groups. This is an area of social studies. So is learning about very early people. So is studying government.

Is social studies important? Early Americans thought so. Students then learned history and civics. This was to make them good citizens. A report from 1916 set a new goal. It said, "The social studies should cultivate a sense of membership in the world community." The world community is very large. But today it is easy to share ideas in it. We have radio and TV. We have phones. We have computers.

Social studies helps us understand the world's people. It helps us know groups and societies. The 1916 goal was important then. It is even more important now. We all need to be good world citizens.

Main Idea	1	Answer	Score
	Mark the *main idea*	M	15
	Mark the statement that is *too broad*	B	5
	Mark the statement that is *too narrow*	N	5

a. Social studies includes many areas of study about people and how they live. ☐ _____

b. A report from 1916 set a new goal for learning social studies. ☐ _____

c. Social studies is an important field. ☐ _____

Score 15 points for each correct answer.   **Score**

Subject Matter **2** Social studies
☐ a. uses radios, TVs, and computers.
☐ b. is the study of people, groups, and societies.
☐ c. can be understood by questioning students.
☐ d. was first taught in 1916. _____

Supporting Details **3** Which fact supports the statement that students did not know geography?
☐ a. A survey questioned 5,000 students.
☐ b. Most students did not know when the Civil War was.
☐ c. Many students did not know World War II leaders.
☐ d. Half of the students from Baltimore could not locate the United States on a map. _____

Conclusion **4** This passage makes it clear that
☐ a. we are not members of a world community.
☐ b. social studies helps make good world citizens.
☐ c. researchers should question more students.
☐ d. social studies is not important. _____

Clarifying Devices **5** The quotation marks around the sentence "the social studies should cultivate a sense of membership in the world community" show that it
☐ a. is important.
☐ b. is the writer's opinion.
☐ c. is the exact words from the 1916 report.
☐ d. was spoken by a high school student. _____

Vocabulary in Context **6** The word <u>survey</u> in this passage means a
☐ a. general look.
☐ b. plan showing size, shape, and boundaries.
☐ c. formal study or poll.
☐ d. discussion. _____

Add your scores for questions 1–6. Enter the total here and on the graph on page 158.   **Total Score** _____

8 The Fertile Crescent

Eleven thousand years ago, the area called the Fertile Crescent may have seemed an unlikely place to live and farm. This flat land in the Middle East was barren and dry. The clay soil was hard. Rain was scarce. So why did one of the first civilizations begin here?

Much of the Fertile Crescent is between two rivers. These are the Tigris and the Euphrates. How could people get the river water to their dry fields? They needed canals, ditches, or pipes to carry water to the dry land. This is called irrigation. With irrigation, people could grow crops.

Irrigation caused farming in the Fertile Crescent to become more successful. Farmers grew many crops. They grew barley, wheat, vegetables, date palms, and grapevines. There was plenty of food. As a result, several things happened.

One result was this: People were no longer hungry. They could store food for times when the crops did not do well.

Another result was that people could have other skills. Not everyone had to be a farmer. People could be gem cutters, metal workers, or carpenters. They could be judges, doctors, or musicians.

And so the population increased. Cities grew. Leaders organized the people. Canals were planned, built, and taken care of. The people needed leaders to get these jobs done.

As time went on, people could trade <u>surplus</u> grain for things they did not grow or make. They could trade for timber, stone, gems, and metals.

All these things made a civilization. That is why this area, the Fertile Crescent, is where one of the world's first civilizations began.

Main Idea	1		
		Answer	Score
Mark the *main idea*		M	15
Mark the statement that is *too broad*		B	5
Mark the statement that is *too narrow*		N	5

a. Successful farming led to one of the world's first civilizations. ☐ _____

b. The Fertile Crescent is between the Tigris and Euphrates Rivers. ☐ _____

c. Civilization depends on farming. ☐

Score 15 points for each correct answer.   **Score**

Subject Matter   2   This passage is mainly about
- [ ] a. irrigation.
- [ ] b. the beginnings of trade.
- [ ] c. why a civilization like the Fertile Crescent developed.
- [ ] d. the growth of a city.

_____

Supporting Details   3   Farming was successful because
- [ ] a. cities grew.
- [ ] b. the people could learn new trades.
- [ ] c. the people had leaders.
- [ ] d. irrigation brought water to dry land.

_____

Conclusion   4   This passage suggests that
- [ ] a. civilizations can develop anywhere.
- [ ] b. big cities are better than small cities.
- [ ] c. as civilizations grow, they no longer need farms.
- [ ] d. certain conditions are necessary for a civilization.

_____

Clarifying Devices   5   The writer introduces the topic of the passage by
- [ ] a. asking a question in the first paragraph.
- [ ] b. asking a question in the second paragraph.
- [ ] c. defining irrigation.
- [ ] d. listing several results.

_____

Vocabulary in Context   6   The word surplus means
- [ ] a. more than what is needed.
- [ ] b. cheap.
- [ ] c. dry.
- [ ] d. stored in sacks.

_____

Add your scores for questions 1–6. Enter the total here and on the graph on page 158.   **Total Score**

_____

9 "I Will Fight No More Forever"

For centuries the Nez Perce called Oregon's Wallowa Valley home. Then in 1876 the U.S. government ordered this Native American tribe to move to a reservation. A few bands rebelled. These groups began fighting two wars—one with the U.S. Army, the other with nature. The groups needed meat and hides for the coming winter. Stopping to hunt meant risking death at the hands of the pursuing army. Pushing on to the safety of the Canadian border meant death at the hands of nature.

The Nez Perce stopped to hunt on September 30, 1877. Before they could continue on to Canada, their pursuers caught up. They fought all day. When night fell, the Nez Perce dug shelter pits for the women and children. They dug rifle pits for the warriors. Snow fell for five days and nights. The Nez Perce huddled in their pits while rifle bullets and cannon shells rained down on them. On the afternoon of October 5, 1877, Chief Joseph and five warriors approached General Howard of the U.S. Army. After handing over his rifle, Joseph spoke:

"The little children are freezing to death. My people, some of them, have run away to the hills and have no blankets, no food. No one knows where they are—perhaps freezing to death. I want to have time to look for my children and see how many I can find. Maybe I shall find them among the dead. I am tired; my heart is sick and sad. From where the sun now stands, I will fight no more forever."

Joseph was speaking for the Nez Perce that afternoon, but he might have been speaking for all Native Americans. The U.S. government <u>mission</u> to confine the first Americans was now nearly over.

Main Idea	1		Answer	Score
	Mark the *main idea*		M	15
	Mark the statement that is *too broad*		B	5
	Mark the statement that is *too narrow*		N	5

a. The U.S. government had a harsh Indian policy. ☐ _____

b. The U.S. Army pursued the Nez Perce until the Nez Perce could no longer fight. ☐ _____

c. Chief Joseph surrendered to General Howard. ☐ _____

Score 15 points for each correct answer.   **Score**

Subject Matter   **2**   This passage is mainly about
- [ ] a. General Howard and the U.S. Army.
- [ ] b. the Canadians.
- [ ] c. the Nez Perce and Chief Joseph.
- [ ] d. all Native Americans.   _____

Supporting   **3**   The Nez Perce headed for the Canadian border
Details   because
- [ ] a. they were Canadian citizens.
- [ ] b. the hunting was better in Canada.
- [ ] c. they would be safe from the U.S.
          Army there.
- [ ] d. they liked the colder weather.   _____

Conclusion   **4**   What did Chief Joseph mean when he said,
                          "I will fight no more forever"?
- [ ] a. The battle was just beginning.
- [ ] b. He would never again take part in such a
          battle.
- [ ] c. He would continue to fight forever.
- [ ] d. He would stop fighting until he reached
          Canada.   _____

Clarifying   **5**   What do the words "rifle bullets and cannon
Devices   shells rained down on them" tell about the attack?
- [ ] a. The army attack was continual and heavy.
- [ ] b. The Nez Perce were getting very wet.
- [ ] c. The army attack did not harm anyone.
- [ ] d. The Nez Perce avoided the attack.   _____

Vocabulary   **6**   In this passage, the word <u>mission</u> means
in Context
- [ ] a. the headquarters of a religious group.
- [ ] b. something that is missing.
- [ ] c. an error in action or judgment.
- [ ] d. the task or job of a military unit.   _____

Add your scores for questions 1–6. Enter the total here   **Total**
and on the graph on page 158.   **Score**   _____

10 What Is Sociology?

Sociology is the study of people in groups. The scientists who study people are called sociologists. They study people in small groups. These may be families. They study people in larger groups. These may be towns or cities. Sometimes they even study people in very large groups such as whole nations. They try to make sense of human behavior.

Sociologists study what causes groups to form and what happens in the groups. For instance, they may look at ethnic groups and the things that people in these groups do. They may look at behavior in various social classes. They may study the way organizations work. They examine work places. They analyze schools. They look at crime and its causes. They study how groups stay the same. They also study how groups change.

Often sociologists look at the same things other social scientists look at. For instance, sociologists study groups during elections. They ask why a group chooses a candidate. Political scientists study the same group. But they look at something different. They look for voting patterns.

How do sociologists study groups? One way is to make a model. The model is a theory. It tries to explain all societies. Sociologists might look at families. They will try to find a pattern. The pattern helps them to explain all groups.

Another way to study groups is to collect information about them. Sociologists use surveys. They ask questions. They look at statistics. They do scientific research.

Sociology is part of daily life. We know our place in a group. We know who is in our group. We know its rules. Groups vary in size. Two people eating together are a group. A big crowd is a group. Sociologists want to know how groups affect our lives.

Main Idea 1		Answer	Score
Mark the *main idea*		M	15
Mark the statement that is *too broad*		B	5
Mark the statement that is *too narrow*		N	5

		Answer	Score
a.	Sociology is the scientific study of people in groups.	☐	____
b.	Sociology is one of the social studies.	☐	____
c.	Sociologists may study groups by collecting information about them.	☐	____

Subject Matter   **2**   This passage is mostly about
- ☐ a. families.
- ☐ b. the training sociologists get.
- ☐ c. why people in groups often don't get along.
- ☐ d. what sociologists do.
     _____

Supporting Details   **3**   Which of the following statements is true?
- ☐ a. Sociologists choose candidates for elections.
- ☐ b. Sociologists look at how groups change.
- ☐ c. Sociologists only study families.
- ☐ d. Sociologists have found no patterns among groups.
     _____

Conclusion   **4**   The writer of the passage leads you to believe that
- ☐ a. sociology is a hard career to train for.
- ☐ b. human behavior cannot be explained by scientists.
- ☐ c. sociologists are satisfied with making models of groups.
- ☐ d. much of what you do in your life is part of a group.
     _____

Clarifying Devices   **5**   The writer discusses political scientists to show
- ☐ a. how they are different from sociologists.
- ☐ b. that they work harder than sociologists.
- ☐ c. that they and sociologists get similar training.
- ☐ d. that only political scientists create models.
     _____

Vocabulary in Context   **6**   The word <u>model</u> in this passage means a
- ☐ a. theory that describes a process.
- ☐ b. person who poses for photographers.
- ☐ c. small copy of something.
- ☐ d. list of questions.
     _____

Add your scores for questions 1–6. Enter the total here and on the graph on page 158.   **Total Score**   _____

11 Tropical Rain Forests

Perhaps you have not stepped into a tropical rain forest. Perhaps you have not felt its year-round temperatures of 70 to 80 degrees. Perhaps you have not gotten wet in downpours that bring more than 80 inches of rain each year. Perhaps you have not looked up to see a green canopy of leaves that blocks the blue of the sky. Perhaps you have never been there. But the tropical rain forest has come to you.

When you smell coffee, eat a banana, or sprinkle cinnamon on your toast, the rain forest comes to you. Coffee beans, bananas, and cinnamon, along with pineapple, mangoes, and chocolate, are all from the tropical rain forest. Even your chewing gum has its origins there. Chicle, the basis for gum, comes from a rain forest tree.

Tropical rain forests are found in lands near the equator, such as Brazil and Malaysia. They cover about two percent of the earth's surface.

Many medicines are made from plants that grow in the tropical rain forest. These include drugs for headaches, high blood pressure, and heart disease. Researchers think there may be many more remedies in the plants there.

The tropical rain forest holds much of Earth's biological <u>diversity</u>. It has three-fourths of all known species of plants and animals. As many as 30 million different kinds of insects live there too.

But the earth is losing its rain forests. Trees are cut for their lumber. Land is cleared by fire to make way for crops and cattle. An area about the size of West Virginia is deforested each year. When the trees are gone, the plants are gone. The animals will be gone too. Many people are concerned. They believe that the survival of the rain forest is crucial to the survival of our world.

Main Idea	1				Answer	Score
		Mark the *main idea*			M	15
		Mark the statement that is *too broad*			B	5
		Mark the statement that is *too narrow*			N	5

a. Much rain forest land is being deforested each year. ☐ _____

b. Rain forests are interesting places. ☐ _____

c. Tropical rain forests are important to people and the earth. ☐ _____

Score 15 points for each correct answer.   **Score**

Subject Matter 2 This passage is primarily
- ☐ a. an informative article about rain forests.
- ☐ b. a personal narrative about one person's trip to a rain forest.
- ☐ c. a description of the rain forest in Brazil.
- ☐ d. the history of rain forests.   _____

Supporting Details 3 Rain forests are located
- ☐ a. close to deserts.
- ☐ b. near the equator.
- ☐ c. near the South Pole.
- ☐ d. in isolated mountain regions.   _____

Conclusion 4 The last paragraph suggests that
- ☐ a. lumber and cattle come from rain forests.
- ☐ b. there is no hope for rain forests because the trees, plants, and animals are gone.
- ☐ c. West Virginia is a rain forest.
- ☐ d. we will be in trouble if we lose the rain forests.   _____

Clarifying Devices 5 The writer attempts to involve the reader in the first two paragraphs by
- ☐ a. frequently using the word *you.*
- ☐ b. writing from the first-person point of view.
- ☐ c. using many convincing numbers and facts.
- ☐ d. asking the reader many questions.   _____

Vocabulary in Context 6 Diversity means
- ☐ a. area.
- ☐ b. variety.
- ☐ c. desert.
- ☐ d. rain water.   _____

Add your scores for questions 1–6. Enter the total here and on the graph on page 158.   **Total Score** _____

12 An Earthquake's Effect on Japan

At dawn on January 17, 1995, the city of Kobe (KOH bee) was rocked by earthquake <u>tremors</u>. The worst tremor reached 7.2 on the Richter scale. Kobe is Japan's sixth largest city. It is also one of the world's largest ports. Within minutes, Kobe was a disaster area.

How bad was the damage? The earthquake was the worst to hit Japan in 72 years. There were more than 6,000 people dead. More than 35,000 were injured, and nearly 310,000 were left homeless. Some 75,000 buildings were damaged or destroyed. Total damage was estimated at $90 billion.

Were the Japanese prepared for earthquakes? They thought they were. They were expecting a big earthquake to strike one of their major cities. But they did not know when, where, or how big the earthquake would be. Architects and engineers believed they had designed earthquake-proof buildings, transportation, and public services. Kobe's few minutes of earth tremors shattered that belief.

What did people learn from the Kobe earthquake? What happened in Kobe suggests that earthquake hazard was not taken seriously enough. Some people believe that more can be done to reduce damage. They propose the following. More work should be put into quake-proofing buildings. Walls should be built to protect towns on the coast from large waves. Providers of emergency services must be better trained and better prepared. Citizens must be better educated on what to do when an earthquake strikes.

The major barrier to doing more is cost. Japan finds itself trying to balance the cost against the risk of a strong earthquake.

Main Idea	1		
		Answer	Score
	Mark the *main idea*	M	15
	Mark the statement that is *too broad*	B	5
	Mark the statement that is *too narrow*	N	5

a. There are lessons to be learned from the Kobe earthquake. ☐ _____

b. The earthquake in Kobe damaged about 75,000 buildings. ☐ _____

c. Japan has severe earthquakes. ☐ _____

Score 15 points for each correct answer.   Score

Subject Matter   **2**   Which sentence best tells what this passage says?
- [ ] a. Cities can be made earthquake proof.
- [ ] b. More can be done to reduce the damage of earthquakes.
- [ ] c. Earthquakes do not do much damage.
- [ ] d. Nothing can be done to reduce the damage of earthquakes.

_____

Supporting Details   **3**   How many people died in the Kobe earthquake?
- [ ] a. more than 6,000
- [ ] b. about 90 billion
- [ ] c. nearly 310,000
- [ ] d. 72

_____

Conclusion   **4**   Why is more not done to protect cities from earthquakes?
- [ ] a. There never will be another earthquake.
- [ ] b. Engineers do not have the knowledge.
- [ ] c. Protection is very costly.
- [ ] d. No one takes earthquakes seriously.

_____

Clarifying Devices   **5**   The pattern used to develop this passage is
- [ ] a. chronological order.
- [ ] b. personal narrative.
- [ ] c. comparison and contrast.
- [ ] d. question and answer.

_____

Vocabulary in Context   **6**   Tremors are
- [ ] a. long, narrow ditches.
- [ ] b. shakings.
- [ ] c. claps of thunder.
- [ ] d. sirens.

_____

Add your scores for questions 1–6. Enter the total here and on the graph on page 158.   Total Score

_____

13 A Marvel of Engineering

The Aztec Indians built their first temple on an island in 1345 A.D. The island was in the middle of swampy Lake Texcoco. A city grew up around this temple, and the Aztecs called it Tenochtitlan. The name means "Place of the Fruit of the Prickly Pear Cactus." Tenochtitlan was where Mexico City, the capital of Mexico, is today.

The Aztecs were good engineers. A 10-mile-long dike held back part of the lake. It helped to control flooding. The Aztecs built three <u>causeways</u> over the swampy waters to link the city with the lakeshore. The bridges in the causeways could be removed. Then gaps were left that kept enemies from entering the city. Inside the city were canals. They linked all parts of the city. People traveling in canoes used the canals as their roads.

The engineers built stone aqueducts to bring fresh water from the mainland to the city. They also drained parts of Lake Texcoco. On the drained land, they made thousands of swamp gardens. The gardens formed a ring around the city. Ditches that linked the gardens were used to drain and irrigate the land.

Aztec houses had one story and a flat roof. In the middle of the city was a large square. In the square were the emperor's palace and the great temple. When the Spaniards arrived in 1519, about 150,000 people lived in Tenochtitlan.

The riches of the city amazed the Spaniards. They wanted Tenochtitlan for themselves. Between 1519 and 1521, Spaniards, along with native tribes, attacked the city. The Aztecs struggled to keep their city, but they were not successful. Tenochtitlan was captured in April 1521. The invaders pulled down most of the buildings. The Aztec Empire was gone forever.

Main Idea	1		
		Answer	Score
	Mark the *main idea*	M	15
	Mark the statement that is *too broad*	B	5
	Mark the statement that is *too narrow*	N	5

a. Remarkable engineering went into the building of Tenochtitlan. ☐ _____

b. The Aztecs built a city in a lake. ☐ _____

c. The Spaniards defeated the Aztecs in 1521. ☐ _____

Score 15 points for each correct answer. **Score**

Subject Matter   **2**   This passage is mainly about
- ☐ a. the Spanish invasion of Tenochtitlan.
- ☐ b. what Tenochtitlan looked like.
- ☐ c. Aztec gardens.
- ☐ d. important cities in Mexico.   _____

Supporting Details   **3**   In this passage, causeways, bridges, canals, and aqueducts are examples of
- ☐ a. Spanish engineering.
- ☐ b. Aztec wealth.
- ☐ c. Aztec religion.
- ☐ d. Aztec engineering.   _____

Conclusion   **4**   Tenochtitlan had canals rather than dirt roads because
- ☐ a. their engineers could not build roads.
- ☐ b. the emperor lived in the center of the city.
- ☐ c. the people were lazy.
- ☐ d. the land was swampy.   _____

Clarifying Devices   **5**   In the third paragraph, a clue to the meaning of *aqueduct* is
- ☐ a. the word *engineers.*
- ☐ b. the words *bring fresh water.*
- ☐ c. the words *to the city.*
- ☐ d. the word *mainland.*   _____

Vocabulary in Context   **6**   The word <u>causeways</u> means
- ☐ a. reasons.
- ☐ b. railways on stilts.
- ☐ c. raised roads across wet land.
- ☐ d. ferryboats.   _____

Add your scores for questions 1–6. Enter the total here and on the graph on page 158.   **Total Score**   _____

14 What Did Confucius Say?

The time after 771 B.C. was a time of unrest in China. Many great thinkers wanted peace and unity. One of the greatest of these thinkers was Confucius.

Confucius lived from 551 B.C. to 479 B.C. His family was poor but of the noble class. Confucius was a good student. He studied hard. He became one of the world's most successful teachers. He had many ideas on how people should live their lives. He also had beliefs about how governments should rule. His ideas and beliefs make up a <u>code</u> of behavior. This code is called Confucianism.

Here are some of the ideas in the code. Kindness and goodness are very important. People must be sincere, loyal, and respectful. They should act this way especially with their families. Rulers must be wise and good. They should set an example. If rulers are wise and good, then their people will also be wise and good.

Confucius died at the age of 72. During his lifetime, he taught about 3,000 disciples. They believed in his ideas. They continued to teach his ideas. One believer named Mencius spread the ideas throughout China. This happened 100 years after Confucius's death. From then on, Confucianism was popular all over the country.

During the Han dynasty, from 206 B.C. to A.D. 220, the ideas of Confucianism became a part of the way of governing. The Han dynasty combined a strong ruler with Confucian ideas. The rulers in this dynasty led their people by good example. They did not use punishment.

Main Idea 1				
			Answer	Score
Mark the *main idea*			M	15
Mark the statement that is *too broad*			B	5
Mark the statement that is *too narrow*			N	5
a. Ancient China had many great thinkers.			☐	____
b. Confucius was an important Chinese thinker.			☐	____
c. The Han dynasty accepted the ideas of Confucianism.			☐	____

Score 15 points for each correct answer. Score

Subject Matter 2 This passage is mainly about
☐ a. Confucius's life.
☐ b. Confucius's thinking.
☐ c. Chinese government.
☐ d. Chinese mathematics. _____

Supporting Details 3 Confucius taught
☐ a. the rulers of the Han dynasty.
☐ b. Mencius.
☐ c. about 3,000 disciples.
☐ d. all the great Chinese thinkers. _____

Conclusion 4 The Han dynasty ruled China for about
☐ a. 200 years.
☐ b. 400 years.
☐ c. 14 years.
☐ d. 1,000 years. _____

Clarifying Devices 5 The first paragraph of the passage
☐ a. compares Chinese life before and after Confucius.
☐ b. identifies other great Chinese thinkers.
☐ c. shows why the Han dynasty came to power.
☐ d. establishes the background for Confucius's thinking. _____

Vocabulary in Context 6 The word <u>code</u> in this passage means
☐ a. secret writing.
☐ b. a set of signals to send messages.
☐ c. rules of conduct.
☐ d. written laws of a nation. _____

Add your scores for questions 1–6. Enter the total here and on the graph on page 158. Total Score _____

15 What Is Anthropology?

Ancient Greeks observed people that they conquered. Ancient Romans kept records of people on the edges of their empire. What were they doing?

Early Europeans heard about exotic people. They thought about human nature. They wondered what makes us human. They pondered civilization. Explorers traveled to new worlds. They came back with stories of strange people. Missionaries went to unexplored places. They wrote about the new cultures they saw.

Then scientists traveled to these new places. They wanted to study the people for themselves. They lived with the people. They observed their ways of life. Some lived with people along the Amazon. Some lived with islanders. Others lived with the Aborigines. They studied people's physical characteristics. They studied their customs and habits. They got ideas and formed theories. What were these scientists doing?

The scientists were doing anthropology. This is a social science that looks at human beings. It looks at differences between people. It also looks for things that humans share.

Anthropologists often look at people in groups. So in this way they are like sociologists. But generally they look at people in less-developed areas of the world. They may compare life in several of these areas. Or they may compare one group with a more-developed culture. They learn that some people have very unusual customs and beliefs. They learn also that some things are the same everywhere. Parents love their children. Families are important. People select leaders. It is only *how* these things are done that is different.

Main Idea	1		Answer	Score
	Mark the *main idea*		M	15
	Mark the statement that is *too broad*		B	5
	Mark the statement that is *too narrow*		N	5
	a. People are interested in people.		☐	_____
	b. Anthropology is the study of people.		☐	_____
	c. Scientists traveled to new places to study people.		☐	_____

Score 15 points for each correct answer.   **Score**

Subject Matter 2 This passage is
- ☐ a. an overview of what anthropology is.
- ☐ b. a research study.
- ☐ c. a biography of an anthropologist.
- ☐ d. a personal narrative.   _____

Supporting Details 3 Some of the first people to study other cultures were
- ☐ a. scientists.
- ☐ b. missionaries.
- ☐ c. people along the Amazon.
- ☐ d. ancient Greeks and Romans.   _____

Conclusion 4 The passage suggests that
- ☐ a. some groups hate their children.
- ☐ b. certain basic values are the same in all societies.
- ☐ c. missionaries wanted to be conquerors.
- ☐ d. all people need to be told what to do.   _____

Clarifying Devices 5 The author compares anthropology and sociology to
- ☐ a. show how they are different.
- ☐ b. show why anthropology is a better area to study.
- ☐ c. confuse the reader.
- ☐ d. criticize certain scientists.   _____

Vocabulary in Context 6 The word <u>pondered</u> means
- ☐ a. carefully thought about.
- ☐ b. laughed at.
- ☐ c. explored.
- ☐ d. participated in.   _____

Add your scores for questions 1–6. Enter the total here and on the graph on page 158.   **Total Score**   _____

16 What Do Fossils Tell Us?

One special branch of anthropology is archaeology. Archaeologists are scientists who look at fossil bones and tools. They look at other artifacts from long ago too. They use the fossils to put together a picture of early people. They can tell who people were. They can tell how people lived. Three-million-year-old bones can tell how ancient humans walked. Stone tools help tell what things they made and how they made them. Campfire ashes hold clues to what people ate.

One special discovery was the Neanderthal fossils. The fossils were found in 1856 in the Neander Valley, near Dusseldorf, Germany, by quarrymen. Much fossil information was lost when the site was blasted for its rocks, but something interesting was discovered. Scientists found evidence that these <u>prehistoric</u> people may have cared about each other.

At first scientists thought the fossil evidence showed that Neanderthals stooped over. They thought that they walked with their knees bent. More study showed that Neanderthals actually had arthritis. Arthritis is a crippling disease that caused the older people to bend over. These fossils provide evidence that the Neanderthal people took care of one another. Life millions of years ago was very harsh. Without care, a handicapped person would not have lived to an old age.

The graves had more evidence of caring. One man was buried on a bed of wildflowers. A teenage boy was buried with an ax and food. Perhaps the wildflowers show that someone was sad at the young man's death. Perhaps the ax and food were things it was thought the boy needed for his life after death. Perhaps the Neanderthals were not as limited as scientists first thought.

Main Idea   1

	Answer	Score
Mark the *main idea*	M	15
Mark the statement that is *too broad*	B	5
Mark the statement that is *too narrow*	N	5

a. Wildflowers were found in Neanderthal graves.	☐	_____
b. Fossils give evidence of how Neanderthals lived.	☐	_____
c. Archaeologists are scientists.	☐	_____

Subject Matter　2　This passage is mainly about
- ☐ a. people caring for one another.
- ☐ b. bones found in a quarry.
- ☐ c. what fossils reveal about Neanderthals.
- ☐ d. fossils.

_____

Supporting Details　3　Arthritis caused Neanderthals to
- ☐ a. live to a very old age.
- ☐ b. be crippled and bent over.
- ☐ c. die.
- ☐ d. be buried with wildflowers.

_____

Conclusion　4　The final paragraph suggests that
- ☐ a. very few prehistoric peoples cared for one another.
- ☐ b. most Neanderthals died young.
- ☐ c. wildflowers grew everywhere during the Neanderthal era.
- ☐ d. archaeologists are not always right.

_____

Clarifying Devices　5　The first paragraph of this passage
- ☐ a. introduces the Neanderthal people.
- ☐ b. asks a question that will be answered in the passage.
- ☐ c. tells what archaeologists think about prehistoric life.
- ☐ d. defines the job of an archaeologist.

_____

Vocabulary in Context　6　Prehistoric means
- ☐ a. the time before written history.
- ☐ b. gentle.
- ☐ c. anxious and tense.
- ☐ d. from a historical and important time.

_____

Add your scores for questions 1–6. Enter the total here and on the graph on page 158.　　**Total Score**　_____

17 Renaissance: A Rebirth of Thinking

The word *Renaissance* (REN uh sahns) comes from a French word meaning "rebirth." It is the time in Europe from the 1300s to the late 1500s. This was a time of the rebirth of ancient Roman ideas. It was also a time of new ideas.

The invention of the printing press was crucial in spreading Renaissance ideas. The new movable type press was first used in Europe in 1455. Before then most books had been copied by hand. Some were printed from carved wooden blocks. The new press made it possible to print books quickly and cheaply. Books and pamphlets became more available to everyone. More people knew how to read than ever before.

Renaissance people began to think learning was important. Wealthy people and artists explored new ideas. Scientists studied medicine and physics. They studied mathematics. They made new discoveries. Humanists had ideas about how to solve society's problems. They had ideas about how to care for fellow human beings.

The Renaissance had another side too. Some people studied magic and astrology. Some people were punished for being witches. Some said society was evil and corrupt. Others wanted governments to be more fair. Others protested the church. They said its leaders were concerned more with money and power than with religion. This was the dark side of the Renaissance.

The end of the Renaissance did not come at any one point. It ended at different times in different countries. It ended when political and church leaders no longer supported the new ideas. It ended when those in power feared that new learning would lead to dangerous thinking.

Main Idea	1		Answer	Score
	Mark the *main idea*		M	15
	Mark the statement that is *too broad*		B	5
	Mark the statement that is *too narrow*		N	5

a. Renaissance scientists made new discoveries. ☐ _____

b. The Renaissance was a period of new thinking and ideas. ☐ _____

c. The Renaissance was a period in Europe. ☐ _____

Score 15 points for each correct answer. **Score**

Subject Matter 2 Another good title for this passage would be
☐ a. The Importance of Making Books.
☐ b. A Period More Evil than Good.
☐ c. Many Scientists and Artists.
☐ d. A Time of New Ideas. _____

Supporting Details 3 What Renaissance invention made it possible to quickly print books?
☐ a. the wheel
☐ b. the printing press
☐ c. paper
☐ d. written language _____

Conclusion 4 What led to the end of the Renaissance?
☐ a. printing presses no longer being used
☐ b. the acceptance of magic and witches
☐ c. the beginning of the sixteenth century
☐ d. a fear of new ideas _____

Clarifying Devices 5 The writer explains the meaning of *Renaissance* through
☐ a. personal narrative.
☐ b. an explanation of the printing press.
☐ c. definition and examples.
☐ d. question and answer. _____

Vocabulary in Context 6 In this passage, the word <u>humanists</u> means
☐ a. people concerned with the study of human interests.
☐ b. people who read books and pamphlets.
☐ c. people who sing with closed lips.
☐ d. all leaders of the church. _____

Add your scores for questions 1–6. Enter the total here and on the graph on page 158. **Total Score** _____

18 What Is Political Science?

Political science is the study of power. It looks at how governments use power. It looks at how individuals use power. It looks at how groups control each other.

Political scientists want to know how nations are governed. They want to know how social groups are organized. They ask, "How do institutions work?"

One tool political scientists use is public opinion polls. Political scientists look at how voters influence public policy. They ask, "Which groups influence elections?" They look at the demands of interest groups. They ask, "How do groups influence laws?" Political scientists also look at the impact of <u>mass media</u>. They want to know what role the media play. They ask, "How do TV, radio, newspapers, and books change people's views?"

Political scientists want to know about nations. They ask questions like the following. How do nations cooperate? What are the ties between them? How do conflicts emerge? How are conflicts resolved? Political scientists also compare political systems. They try to find out who depends on whom. They study international legal systems. They study agreements between nations.

During the 1960s, political science changed. The 1960s were a time of disagreement. Before then much of political science was theory. But during that time, many political scientists turned to issues. Scholars wanted to deal with values and facts. They got involved with the Vietnam War. They looked at causes for inner city riots. They examined the impact of assassinations.

Today theory blends with values. Topics such as peace, justice, and human rights are discussed. These values are now part of the study of political science.

Main Idea	1		
		Answer	Score
	Mark the *main idea*	M	15
	Mark the statement that is *too broad*	B	5
	Mark the statement that is *too narrow*	N	5
	a. Political science is a course of study.	☐	____
	b. Political science is the study of how governments and groups use power.	☐	____
	c. Political science began examining issues in the 1960s.	☐	____

Score 15 points for each correct answer.   Score

Subject Matter   2 Another good title for this passage is
    □ a. How to Become a Political Scientist.
    □ b. What Political Scientists Want to Know.
    □ c. Political Science in the 1960s.
    □ d. Political Science and Television.   _____

Supporting   3 Public opinion polls help political scientists
Details   understand
    □ a. how people fill out surveys.
    □ b. how voters influence public policy.
    □ c. international legal systems.
    □ d. how peace can be achieved.   _____

Conclusion   4 What conclusion can the reader draw from the
                       many questions asked in this passage?
    □ a. Very little is known about political science.
    □ b. Political scientists ask many questions in
                          their search for knowledge.
    □ c. Political scientists have all the answers.
    □ d. The reader should know the answers to
                          these questions.   _____

Clarifying   5 In the repeated phrase "they ask" in this passage,
Devices   *they* refers to
    □ a. governments.
    □ b. voters.
    □ c. political scientists.
    □ d. public opinion polls.   _____

Vocabulary   6 The term mass media means
in Context
    □ a. interest groups.
    □ b. voters.
    □ c. personal letters, diaries, journals.
    □ d. TV, radio, newspapers, books.   _____

Add your scores for questions 1–6. Enter the total here   Total
and on the graph on page 158.   Score   _____

19 Bessie Coleman, Determined Pilot

For the first 10 years after the Wright brothers' original flight in 1903, flying was only a sport. It was a pastime for daredevils. One very determined daredevil was Bessie Coleman. She was the first black woman to fly an airplane.

Coleman, born in Texas in 1892, the tenth of 13 children, dreamed of being a pilot. To earn money for flying lessons, she washed other people's laundry. At the age of 19, she took a train to Chicago, where she enrolled in a beauty school. For five years, she worked in a barbershop, and then she looked for a flying school. No flying schools in the United States would teach women, but Coleman heard that there were schools in France that would. So she studied French and sailed off to France.

When she returned to the United States in 1921, Coleman was the first licensed black woman pilot. Her "aerial acrobatic <u>exhibitions</u>" dazzled audiences. She took her airplane through loop-the-loops. She did slow rolls and sharp rolls. She did tailspins and flew upside down. Audiences were amazed when she performed a move called "falling leaf."

Coleman became a celebrity. She performed her acrobatic flights all over the country. She also spoke to African-American audiences in schools, churches, and theaters. Fly, she told them. Be a part of the new aviation industry. Many young African-American men listened to her. Some became honored military pilots during World War II. Many others made their careers in aviation.

On April 29, 1926, Coleman was flying when a tool carelessly left in the airplane cockpit jammed the control stick. The plane went into a dive and did not recover. The daring 34-year-old pilot was killed.

Main Idea	1			
			Answer	**Score**
	Mark the *main idea*		M	15
	Mark the statement that is *too broad*		B	5
	Mark the statement that is *too narrow*		N	5
	a.	Many early pilots were daredevils.	☐	_____
	b.	Women could learn to fly in France.	☐	_____
	c.	Bessie Coleman was a pioneer in the aviation industry.	☐	_____

Score 15 points for each correct answer.   **Score**

Subject Matter   2   The focus of this passage is mainly
- ☐ a. French history.
- ☐ b. United States history.
- ☐ c. World War II history.
- ☐ d. aviation history.   _____

Supporting Details   3   Bessie Coleman went to France to
- ☐ a. speak to African-American audiences.
- ☐ b. learn to fly.
- ☐ c. go to beauty school.
- ☐ d. learn French.   _____

Conclusion   4   Bessie Coleman's life teaches which of the following lessons?
- ☐ a. Become a celebrity.
- ☐ b. Flying is a pastime for daredevils.
- ☐ c. Follow your dreams.
- ☐ d. Learn French.   _____

Clarifying Devices   5   Which of the following is an "aerial acrobatic"?
- ☐ a. flying upside down
- ☐ b. speaking to audiences
- ☐ c. getting a pilot's license
- ☐ d. dazzling audiences   _____

Vocabulary in Context   6   The word <u>exhibition</u> means
- ☐ a. a holding back.
- ☐ b. outside of Earth's atmosphere.
- ☐ c. a public show.
- ☐ d. the amount of money spent.   _____

Add your scores for questions 1–6. Enter the total here and on the graph on page 158.   **Total Score**   _____

20 What Is Psychology?

Why do human beings behave as they do? This is something people have always wondered. Aristotle, an ancient Greek thinker, said the mind was separate from the body. He wanted to know what the mind could do. *Psychology* comes from two Greek words. One is *psyche,* meaning "mind." The other is *logia,* meaning "study." So psychology is "the study of the mind."

In the Middle Ages, <u>scholars</u> studied people's behavior from a religious viewpoint. In the 1600s and 1700s, other views became important. Some scholars believed as Aristotle did—that the mind and body are separate. They believed the mind can think and reason at birth. Others said the mind is empty at birth. They said that knowledge comes from the senses and that ideas come from experience.

In the 1800s, German researchers began to study the mind in a scientific way. Then an American set up the first lab where experiments on the mind could be performed. Psychology became its own field of study.

Today psychology is a social science. It studies behavior and the way the mind works. Psychologists observe people, conduct experiments, and record what they see. They look for patterns to help them understand and predict behavior.

When psychologists work with people, they ask questions about thoughts, feelings, and actions. The answers can help people better understand their own personalities. They can help people change habits and sometimes even find ways to learn better. With psychology, we can begin to answer our first question: Why do human beings behave as they do?

Main Idea	1	Answer	Score
		Answer	**Score**
	Mark the *main idea*	M	15
	Mark the statement that is *too broad*	B	5
	Mark the statement that is *too narrow*	N	5
	a. Psychology may be practiced in labs.	☐	_____
	b. Psychology studies the mind and behavior.	☐	_____
	c. Psychology is a social science.	☐	_____

Score 15 points for each correct answer. **Score**

Subject Matter 2 This passage is mostly about
☐ a. psychology and its development.
☐ b. famous people who studied psychology.
☐ c. why psychology is popular today.
☐ d. psychology in the Middle Ages. _____

Supporting Details 3 The first scientific study of the mind was done by
☐ a. Greeks.
☐ b. Americans.
☐ c. Germans.
☐ d. the French. _____

Conclusion 4 To practice psychology correctly, a person should
☐ a. be familiar with research done by others.
☐ b. rely mainly on a desire to help people.
☐ c. have an office with a couch in it.
☐ d. have personal problems that need to be solved. _____

Clarifying Devices 5 The first three paragraphs of this passage
☐ a. give an explanation of psychology.
☐ b. tell the history of psychology.
☐ c. show how psychology helps people.
☐ d. ask questions about psychology. _____

Vocabulary in Context 6 In this passage, a <u>scholar</u> is someone
☐ a. who owns a school.
☐ b. from Nova Scotia.
☐ c. with a lot of knowledge.
☐ d. who works for the church. _____

Add your scores for questions 1–6. Enter the total here and on the graph on page 158. **Total Score** _____

41

21 The First Written Records

No computers, no calculators, no paper and pencil. Before writing, people's memories were the containers for storing knowledge. But in ancient Mesopotamia, the Sumerians were about to invent the first writing. The time was more than 4,000 years ago.

Many Sumerians were merchants and traders. They traded grain, dates, wool, and dairy products for tools and building supplies. The Sumerians needed to keep track of all this trading. At first they used clay or stone tokens in a clay jar called a *bulla*. The marks they made on the outside of the bulla may have led to the invention of writing. Their first written symbols were pictures of the things they traded. Later, the pictures stood for syllables. Soon the Sumerians were combining those syllables into words.

Around 3000 B.C., the pictures were drawn more simply. Another type of writing <u>emerged</u> called cuneiform. This writing could be done easily on wet clay. The marks were written in the clay with a narrow reed or stick and were shaped like a triangle. Cuneiform had 600 symbols. With cuneiform, people could record the histories of the wars they fought. They could even write poems. Cuneiform was used in the Middle East for about 2,000 years.

Modern people could not read cuneiform. But in the 1800s, an important translation was made by Sir Henry Creswicke Rawlinson. He translated some ancient writing that was found in Iran. His translation led to an understanding of ancient cuneiform. Archaeologists today continue to translate the first writings. Each translation gives more information about ancient people.

Main Idea	1			
			Answer	**Score**
	Mark the *main idea*		M	15
	Mark the statement that is *too broad*		B	5
	Mark the statement that is *too narrow*		N	5
	a.	The Sumerians were an ancient people.	☐	_____
	b.	The Sumerians traded items like grain and wool.	☐	_____
	c.	The first writing was invented by the Sumerians.	☐	_____

Subject Matter   **2**   This passage is mostly about
- ☐ a. Sumerian culture.
- ☐ b. the development of early writing.
- ☐ c. why trade was important in ancient civilizations.
- ☐ d. Sir Henry Creswicke Rawlinson.   _____

Supporting Details   **3**   Cuneiform contained
- ☐ a. pictures of things that were traded.
- ☐ b. an alphabet similar to the one we use today.
- ☐ c. syllables and words.
- ☐ d. about 600 symbols.   _____

Conclusion   **4**   Writing developed because people
- ☐ a. wanted to read books.
- ☐ b. had a need to keep records.
- ☐ c. were not good at drawing pictures.
- ☐ d. had poor memories.   _____

Clarifying Devices   **5**   In the first paragraph, "people's memories were the containers for storing knowledge" is
- ☐ a. a simile.
- ☐ b. a metaphor.
- ☐ c. a rhyme.
- ☐ d. personification.   _____

Vocabulary in Context   **6**   The word <u>emerged</u> means
- ☐ a. went under.
- ☐ b. needed help.
- ☐ c. came forth.
- ☐ d. vanished.   _____

Add your scores for questions 1–6. Enter the total here and on the graph on page 158.   **Total Score**   _____

22 The Beginnings of Democracy

Democracy, or rule by all the people, is often upheld as an <u>ideal</u> form of government. Democracy began in ancient Greece, but it developed slowly.

Before there was democracy, the people of Greece came under other forms of rule. First there was monarchy, in which a king ruled over the people. During the Dark Age of Greece, most Greek city-states were monarchies. Next there was oligarchy. Here a small group of people ruled over everyone else. At the end of the Dark Age, a small group of nobles shared power with the king. Then during the sixth century B.C., there were problems with oligarchies. This led to the rise of tyrants. Even though tyrants seized power by force, the Greek people supported them. The tyrants promised to reform laws and help the poor. Finally, in about 510 B.C., the people had had enough of tyrants. They threw the tyrants out of power. The people decided to share the power. This was the beginning of democracy.

In the democratic city of Athens, Greece, citizens took part in the government. Not everyone, though, could be a citizen. A citizen had to be a male over the age of 18. Usually a man's father, and sometimes his mother's father, also had to be citizens. Only about 15 percent of the 300,000 people living in Athens could be citizens. Women and children could not be citizens, even though they made up 48 percent of the population. Foreigners living in Athens could not be citizens, even though they made up 12 percent of the population. Slaves could not be citizens, even though they made up 25 percent of the population.

The democracy of the ancient Greeks is not the ideal for which modern countries strive. But the Greeks can take credit for the beginning of an idea.

Main Idea	1	Answer	Score
	Mark the *main idea*	M	15
	Mark the statement that is *too broad*	B	5
	Mark the statement that is *too narrow*	N	5
	a. Democracy began in Greece.	☐	___
	b. Oligarchies led to democracy.	☐	___
	c. Democracy is a form of government.	☐	___

Subject Matter 2 This passage is mainly about
☐ a. the beginnings of democracy.
☐ b. all forms of government.
☐ c. Greek life.
☐ d. oligarchies. _____

Supporting Details 3 People supported tyrants because
☐ a. they were tired of being ruled by a king.
☐ b. tyrants promised democratic rule.
☐ c. tyrants made promises of reform.
☐ d. women could now vote. _____

Conclusion 4 Which statement best summarizes the ideas in this passage?
☐ a. Democracy began in Europe.
☐ b. Democracy caught on quickly everywhere.
☐ c. Early Greek democracy was for all people.
☐ d. The true ideal of democracy was begun but not achieved in ancient Greece. _____

Clarifying Devices 5 The order of ancient Greek governments is indicated by
☐ a. a timeline.
☐ b. the numerals 1, 2, 3, and 4.
☐ c. the words *first, next, then,* and *finally.*
☐ d. a bulleted list. _____

Vocabulary in Context 6 The word <u>ideal</u> in this passage means
☐ a. expensive.
☐ b. perfect.
☐ c. unusual.
☐ d. a thought. _____

Add your scores for questions 1–6. Enter the total here and on the graph on page 158. **Total Score** _____

23 The Unmaking of an Anthropology Myth

Anthropologist Margaret Mead (1901–1978) said people in the United States could learn from the Samoans about raising children. What she had to say in her popular book *Coming of Age in Samoa* (1928) shocked people of her time. Mead, a young anthropologist in 1925–1926, studied the Samoan people. In Samoa, she said, life is free and easy. Samoa, she said, has no violence, no guilt, no anger. Samoan teens do not feel the pressures teens in the United States feel. In Samoa, she wrote, families are large and taboos are few. Disagreements are easily settled.

Years after Mead's book was published, Australian researcher Derek Freeman disagreed. In 1983 he published *Margaret Mead and Samoa: The Making and Unmaking of an Anthropological Myth.* His own work in Samoa got very different results. He says Mead ignored facts to prove a theory. That theory proposes that culture, not biology, has the greatest influence on growing up.

Freeman also says Mead did not correctly interpret her data. He says she did not understand how the Samoans really felt toward relationships. He claims that two girls she talked to told her "stories." He says Mead was <u>duped</u> into believing these untrue stories. Also, Mead told of a Samoan life of leisure, living on the beach, without stress. Freeman said this was a fantasy. He researched Samoan crime statistics and history. The 1920s in Samoa, he says, were a time of violence.

In spite of these doubts about her first work, Mead left behind a lifetime of important contributions to the understanding of human history.

Main Idea	1	Answer	Score
	Mark the *main idea*	M	15
	Mark the statement that is *too broad*	B	5
	Mark the statement that is *too narrow*	N	5

a. Anthropological studies have been conducted in Samoa. ☐ _____

b. Derek Freeman claims that Margaret Mead's research in Samoa was incorrectly interpreted. ☐ _____

c. Margaret Mead went to Samoa in 1925. ☐ _____

Subject Matter   **2**   This passage is mostly about
- ☐ a. Mead's work and Freeman's disagreement with it.
- ☐ b. Samoan society in the 1980s.
- ☐ c. Australian society in the 1980s.
- ☐ d. Margaret Mead's early upbringing.   ____

Supporting Details   **3**   Derek Freeman's book was published
- ☐ a. 20 years after Mead's book.
- ☐ b. 55 years before Mead's book.
- ☐ c. 2 to 3 years after Mead's book.
- ☐ d. 55 years after Mead's book.   ____

Conclusion   **4**   The final paragraph suggests that
- ☐ a. Mead spent her life studying, writing about, and contributing to anthropology.
- ☐ b. other work Mead did in her lifetime was unimportant.
- ☐ c. all of Mead's work has been questioned.
- ☐ d. Mead's research stopped with *Coming of Age in Samoa*.   ____

Clarifying Devices   **5**   The basic pattern used to develop this passage is
- ☐ a. personal narrative.
- ☐ b. question and answer.
- ☐ c. spatial description.
- ☐ d. statement and disagreement.   ____

Vocabulary in Context   **6**   The word <u>duped</u> in this passage means
- ☐ a. copied.
- ☐ b. paid.
- ☐ c. deceived or tricked.
- ☐ d. confused.   ____

Add your scores for questions 1–6. Enter the total here and on the graph on page 158.   **Total Score**   ____

24 Chinese Waterways

China has many natural barriers, including <u>vast</u> mountains, deserts, and oceans that separate its regions. These natural barriers make travel and communication difficult, but from earliest times people have taken advantage of the rivers. Farmers who lived inland used the rivers as roads. They sent their crops on boats to ocean ports. The rivers also provided water for people, animals, and crops. The sandy soil along the banks of the rivers gave them good farmland.

The Chang, or Yangtze, is China's longest river. It is the third longest river in the world. Many cities along the Chang River are important river ports. This river handles about 80 percent of China's inland water traffic. The Chang River is a main waterway connecting eastern and western China.

The Huang, or Yellow, is China's second longest river. It is the fifth longest river in the world. Its brownish-yellow water gave it its name. Before 1949, the Huang River often flooded, causing damage. Now, after 40 years of building river controls such as dikes, the Huang is more predictable.

China's Grand Canal is the world's oldest and longest man-made waterway. It is more than 1,000 miles long. The canal was begun in the sixth century B.C. It was completed in the 13th century A.D. The Grand Canal links several rivers, including the Chang and the Huang. Before railroads were built, it served as the main travel route between northern and southern China.

The canal, like China's rivers, is still in use today. China's waterways continue to carry goods and people. They help connect China's vast regions. In many ways, they are China's lifelines.

Main Idea	1		
		Answer	**Score**
	Mark the *main idea*	M	15
	Mark the statement that is *too broad*	B	5
	Mark the statement that is *too narrow*	N	5

a.	Waterways are important to Chinese life.	☐	_____
b.	Goods are transported on the Grand Canal.	☐	_____
c.	Rivers help countries to develop.	☐	_____

Subject Matter   **2**   Another good title for this passage would be
- ☐ a. Two Chinese Rivers.
- ☐ b. A Short History of China.
- ☐ c. A Transportation System Built on Water.
- ☐ d. The Importance of the Grand Canal.

_____

Supporting Details   **3**   China's longest river is the
- ☐ a. Chang.
- ☐ b. Yellow.
- ☐ c. Grand.
- ☐ d. Huang.

_____

Conclusion   **4**   In earlier times, living very close to the Huang River was
- ☐ a. smart.
- ☐ b. required if you were a trader.
- ☐ c. done only by the very old.
- ☐ d. dangerous.

_____

Clarifying Devices   **5**   The rivers are called "lifelines" in the final paragraph because
- ☐ a. they are places where people can fish.
- ☐ b. boats on them are pulled by ropes.
- ☐ c. they provide vital communication and transport services.
- ☐ d. they are long and narrow.

_____

Vocabulary in Context   **6**   The word vast means
- ☐ a. quick.
- ☐ b. huge.
- ☐ c. changing.
- ☐ d. worthless.

_____

Add your scores for questions 1–6. Enter the total here and on the graph on page 158.   **Total Score**

_____

25 Fewer Births, Longer Lives

Population change depends mainly on a country's birth and death rates. These rates are expressed as the number of births and deaths for every 1,000 people in a year. The difference between the birth rate and the death rate gives the natural increase or decrease of population.

Take the case of Italy, whose population today is about 57$^1/_2$ million. The population increased slowly during most of the twentieth century. By 1996, though, the increase had almost stopped. Italy now has a birth rate of 10 per thousand and a death rate of 10 per thousand, so the natural change is zero. Italy has zero population growth.

Italy's lower death rate is mainly because of better medical care. Fewer babies die, and people now live longer. The average life expectancy in Italy is age 75 for males and age 81 for females.

Italy's lower birth rate has several causes. One cause is that in the 1970s an increase in unemployment left people feeling financially insecure. They chose to have fewer children. Another cause is that more people moved from rural to urban areas. Living and raising children in the city was more costly, so people had fewer children. A third reason is that more women now have careers outside of the home. They choose to have fewer children. And many more children now live at home until they are about 30 years old. They marry later and might not have children at all. A final reason is that many adults want a lifestyle that is not <u>compatible</u> with raising big families.

There is speculation that Italy's growth rate will be less than zero and that the total population will start to decline. It is possible that in 100 years' time there will only be 19 million people living in Italy.

Main Idea	1		Answer	Score
		Mark the *main idea*	**M**	**15**
		Mark the statement that is *too broad*	**B**	**5**
		Mark the statement that is *too narrow*	**N**	**5**
		a. Populations may increase or decrease.	☐	_____
		b. Italy has achieved zero population growth for a variety of reasons.	☐	_____
		c. Italy has a birth rate of 10 per thousand.	☐	_____

Score 15 points for each correct answer. Score

Subject Matter 2 This passage is mostly about
- ☐ a. what zero population growth means.
- ☐ b. why many Italian women work.
- ☐ c. what Italy's population will be in the future.
- ☐ d. why Italy has zero population growth. _____

Supporting Details 3 The yearly death rate in Italy is
- ☐ a. zero.
- ☐ b. 10 per 1,000.
- ☐ c. $57^{1}/_{2}$ million.
- ☐ d. 1,000 a year. _____

Conclusion 4 The passage shows that there is no one single reason for
- ☐ a. Italy's lower death rate.
- ☐ b. Italy's lower birth rate.
- ☐ c. Italy's present employment situation.
- ☐ d. the policies of Italy's government. _____

Clarifying Devices 5 Information about Italy's birth rate is made clearer by the use of
- ☐ a. long sentences.
- ☐ b. stories about women in the workplace.
- ☐ c. transitional words and phrases.
- ☐ d. a bulleted list. _____

Vocabulary in Context 6 The word <u>compatible</u> means
- ☐ a. in agreement.
- ☐ b. understandable.
- ☐ c. legal.
- ☐ d. valued. _____

Add your scores for questions 1–6. Enter the total here and on the graph on page 158. Total Score _____

26 Gold and Silver Worth $30 Million

The Spanish explorer Francisco Pizarro was exploring South America in the 1530s when he saw a large raft. It carried silver, gold, emeralds, and rich cloth. This was his first look at the riches of the Inca Empire. Once this empire covered much of western South America.

Atahualpa was ruler of the Inca Empire. One of his messengers visited Pizarro's camp and invited Pizarro to visit the city of Cajamarca. Pizarro and his men were looking for glory and gold. They wanted to expand the Spanish Empire. So Pizarro and about 160 horsemen and soldiers accepted the invitation. They set off into the Andes Mountains. When Pizarro and his men came out of the mountains, they looked down on Cajamarca Valley. The tents of the Inca army were below them.

To greet Pizarro, Atahualpa had put on embroidered clothes and an emerald collar. He was carried on a special throne to Cajamarca's central square. He arrived with about 5,000 men. Without warning, the Spaniards attacked. The unarmed Inca soldiers tried to escape, but the Spaniards killed thousands of them. They captured Atahualpa.

Atahualpa's people tried to get him back. They gathered gold and silver worth 30 million dollars to give to Pizarro. It was one of the largest ransoms in history. Pizarro agreed to the ransom. But then he did not keep his promise. Instead he accused Atahualpa of sending for an army. The Spaniards sentenced him to death. He was executed in Cajamarca Square.

Pizarro's stolen treasure was 11 tons of gold objects. He melted down almost all of it. Few gold objects survived the Spanish conquest.

Main Idea	1		
		Answer	Score
	Mark the *main idea*	M	15
	Mark the statement that is *too broad*	B	5
	Mark the statement that is *too narrow*	N	5

a. The Spanish explorers stole from and conquered the Incas. ☐ _____

b. Pizarro met the Inca ruler in a public square. ☐ _____

c. The Spanish explored South America. ☐ _____

Score 15 points for each correct answer.   **Score**

Subject Matter   **2**   Another good title for this passage is
     ☐ a. A Meeting in the Andes.
     ☐ b. The Wealth of the Incas.
     ☐ c. The Fall of an Inca Leader.
     ☐ d. Atahualpa and His 5,000 Men.   _____

Supporting   **3**   The value of the ransom was
Details
     ☐ a. paid mostly in emeralds.
     ☐ b. 11 million dollars.
     ☐ c. 30 million dollars.
     ☐ d. 5,000 dollars.   _____

Conclusion   **4**   This passage clearly demonstrates Pizarro's
     ☐ a. bad temper.
     ☐ b. honesty.
     ☐ c. greed.
     ☐ d. fairness.   _____

Clarifying   **5**   The basic pattern used to develop this passage is
Devices
     ☐ a. question and answer.
     ☐ b. a spatial description.
     ☐ c. comparison and contrast.
     ☐ d. chronological order.   _____

Vocabulary   **6**   The word <u>ransoms</u> means
in Context
     ☐ a. prices paid for someone's release.
     ☐ b. searches.
     ☐ c. agreements between two people.
     ☐ d. gatherings of military troops.   _____

Add your scores for questions 1–6. Enter the total here   **Total**
and on the graph on page 159.   **Score**   _____

27 Not Just a White Man's War

President Abraham Lincoln's first call for volunteers to fight in the Civil War was for whites only. The Civil War was a white man's war, northern whites insisted. Its purpose was to preserve the Union. It was not being fought to end slavery. But by September of 1862, the <u>sentiment</u> toward black volunteers had changed. Lincoln had hoped that the war would be short, but it had already lasted nearly a year and a half. Union manpower had fallen dangerously low.

Lincoln had a plan. He issued the Emancipation Proclamation. It stated that as of January 1, 1863, all slaves residing in the rebellious Southern states would be forever free. And starting immediately, Union armies would accept black volunteers.

The Southern Rebels' response to Lincoln's call for black troops was a deadly one. Captives of any Union regiment with black troops were to be given "no quarter." They were to be put to death immediately.

African-American troops throughout the war distinguished themselves in battle at places like Milliken's Bend, Fort Wagner, and the Crater at St. Petersburg. As to their conduct on the battlefield, Colonel Thomas Wentworth Higginson wrote: "Nobody knows anything about these men who has not seen them in battle. No officer in this regiment now doubts that the successful prosecution of the war lies in the unlimited employment of black troops." By the war's end, 186,000 black troops had participated. They made up nearly 10 percent of Union forces. These black soldiers saw action in more than 250 battles. Black soldiers also gave their lives. By the war's end, about 38,000 black troops had died. They had died from battle wounds, disease, and treatment during captivity.

Main Idea	1	Answer	Score
	Mark the *main idea*	M	15
	Mark the statement that is *too broad*	B	5
	Mark the statement that is *too narrow*	N	5

a. Abraham Lincoln's first call for Union troops was for whites only. ☐ ____

b. African-American troops played an important part in the Civil War. ☐ ____

c. Many men served in the Civil War. ☐ ____

Score 15 points for each correct answer.   **Score**

Subject Matter   **2** This passage is mainly about
    ☐ a. causes of the Civil War.
    ☐ b. the Emancipation Proclamation.
    ☐ c. black soldiers in the Civil War.
    ☐ d. why Lincoln was a good President.   _____

Supporting   **3** Feelings about having black volunteers in the
Details   Union army changed because
    ☐ a. Colonel Higginson changed everyone's mind.
    ☐ b. Union captives were being put to death.
    ☐ c. there were not enough Union troops.
    ☐ d. slavery had ended.   _____

Conclusion   **4** The writer of this passage wants the reader to reach
the conclusion that
    ☐ a. Lincoln acted too late to free the slaves.
    ☐ b. blacks fought well for the Union cause.
    ☐ c. the Civil War changed American history.
    ☐ d. the South nearly won the Civil War.   _____

Clarifying   **5** Which sentence from the passage helps clarify the
Devices   phrase *no quarter*?
    ☐ a. They were to be put to death immediately.
    ☐ b. Black troops throughout the war distin-
         guished themselves.
    ☐ c. Nobody knows anything about these men.
    ☐ d. Union armies would accept black volunteers.   _____

Vocabulary   **6** The word <u>sentiment</u> means
in Context   ☐ a. newspaper editorials.
    ☐ b. people who keep watch.
    ☐ c. poetry.
    ☐ d. thought and feeling.   _____

Add your scores for questions 1–6. Enter the total here   **Total**
and on the graph on page 159.   **Score**   _____

28 Pavlov's Bewitched Dogs

Is behavior learned? Psychologists have discussed this question for years. They began thinking about it because of the work of Ivan Pavlov. He was a Russian professor of physiology. Here is his story.

In carefully controlled experiments, Pavlov showed that dogs could be taught to salivate. Critics said the dogs were bewitched. And Pavlov was probably as surprised as his critics. But the evidence was there.

The discovery was accidental. Pavlov was doing research on digestion and on the central nervous system. For his research, he collected saliva from the animals in his laboratory. To get the saliva, he had an experimenter put meat powder in the laboratory dogs' mouths. The meat powder was a stimulus to get the dogs' mouths to water. Soon he noticed that the dogs' mouths watered even before they got the meat powder. In fact, their mouths began to water at the sight of the experimenter. The experimenter had become the stimulus!

Pavlov wondered if other stimuli could get the dogs to salivate. He paired the meat powder with the sound of a tuning fork, the turning on of a light, and the ringing of a bell. He got the same results. An automatic physical response, called a *reflex*, is one of the most basic actions animals perform. Sneezing in a dusty place and shivering in the cold are reflex actions. But Pavlov's experiments showed that reflexes could be taught. This led the way to further thinking on whether behavior is natural or learned.

It may not sound so <u>incredible</u> today, but at the turn of the 20th century Pavlov's research seemed remarkable. It brought about new research methods and ideas. Pavlov continued his work on the nervous system of the dog. He experimented with different stimuli. His work became the basis for much of modern psychology.

Main Idea	1		Answer	Score
	Mark the *main idea*		M	15
	Mark the statement that is *too broad*		B	5
	Mark the statement that is *too narrow*		N	5
	a. Ivan Pavlov was a Russian scientist.		☐	_____
	b. Pavlov's dogs salivated to such stimuli as bells and lights.		☐	_____
	c. Pavlov's experiments led to important psychological findings.		☐	_____

Subject Matter   2   This passage is mostly about
- [ ] a. experiments with different kinds of dogs.
- [ ] b. the meaning of *salivate*.
- [ ] c. how Ivan Pavlov's work with stimuli changed ideas about behavior.
- [ ] d. the life of Ivan Pavlov.   _____

Supporting Details   3   Pavlov's dogs responded to
- [ ] a. newspapers.
- [ ] b. the sound of a bell.
- [ ] c. forks, knives, and spoons.
- [ ] d. saliva.   _____

Conclusion   4   From this passage, it is reasonable to conclude that
- [ ] a. bells should be rung at meal times.
- [ ] b. Pavlov enjoyed being a famous person.
- [ ] c. dogs can be taught to do anything.
- [ ] d. Pavlov became more interested in dogs' brains than in their digestion.   _____

Clarifying Devices   5   People said the dogs were bewitched because
- [ ] a. Pavlov seemed like an evil wizard.
- [ ] b. the dogs were salivating without a direct stimulus.
- [ ] c. the dogs performed in a circus sideshow.
- [ ] d. the dogs never slept after Pavlov's experiment.   _____

Vocabulary in Context   6   The word incredible means
- [ ] a. unpleasant.
- [ ] b. new.
- [ ] c. confusing.
- [ ] d. unbelievable.   _____

Add your scores for questions 1–6. Enter the total here and on the graph on page 159.   Total Score   _____

29 Where in the World?

You probably know your postal address and your zip code, right? But did you know that you can pinpoint your global address too? For example, the global address for downtown Chicago, Illinois, looks like this: 41°50'N 87°45'W. These numbers and symbols tell the latitude and longitude of the city.

Lines of latitude and longitude are the imaginary grid geographers use to locate places on the earth. Latitude is the position of a point on the earth's surface in relation to the equator. The distance is measured in degrees beginning at the equator and going toward one of the earth's poles. Any point on the equator has a latitude of zero degrees. This is written 0°. The North Pole has a latitude of 90° north, and the South Pole has a latitude of 90° south. So a point halfway between the North Pole and the equator would be located at 45 degrees north (45°N). The distance between degrees is divided into 60 minutes. The symbol for minutes is '. So a latitude of 48°40'N would be between 48° and 49° north.

Lines of longitude are imaginary lines running north and south. They divide the globe into 360 equal slices. The main lines of longitude are called meridians. All meridians pass through the North and the South Poles. The <u>prime</u> meridian, or first meridian, is the imaginary line that runs from the North Pole to the South Pole and passes through Greenwich, England, just outside London. This line is 0° longitude. The prime meridian divides the earth into an eastern hemisphere and a western hemisphere. Each hemisphere has 180 degrees. Similar to latitude, each degree of longitude is divided into 60 minutes. The distance between meridians is greatest at the equator; it gradually decreases as the meridians near the poles.

So now, can you find your global address? Where in the world are YOU?

Main Idea	1		Answer	Score
	Mark the *main idea*		M	15
	Mark the statement that is *too broad*		B	5
	Mark the statement that is *too narrow*		N	5

a.	Locations on the earth can be pinpointed by latitude and longitude.	☐	_____
b.	Every place has an address.	☐	_____
c.	Global distances are measured in degrees.	☐	_____

Subject Matter 2 The information in this passage would most
likely be found in a
☐ a. psychology book.
☐ b. sociology book.
☐ c. world history book.
☐ d. geography book. _____

Supporting 3 The equator is at
Details ☐ a. 0° latitude.
☐ b. 45°N latitude.
☐ c. 45°S latitude.
☐ d. 180° latitude. _____

Conclusion 4 A latitude of 75°20'S would be closest to
☐ a. the South Pole.
☐ b. the North Pole.
☐ c. the Equator.
☐ d. Canada. _____

Clarifying 5 The example 41°50'N 87°45'W is an address
Devices ☐ a. for the suburban areas of Chicago.
☐ b. showing latitude only.
☐ c. showing longitude only.
☐ d. showing both latitude and longitude. _____

Vocabulary 6 In this passage, the word <u>prime</u> means
in Context ☐ a. flat.
☐ b. most important.
☐ c. first.
☐ d. long. _____

Add your scores for questions 1–6. Enter the total here **Total**
and on the graph on page 159. **Score** _____

30 Shirley Chisholm, Political Trailblazer

"I stand before you today as a candidate for the Democratic <u>nomination</u> for the presidency of the United States. I am not the candidate of black America, although I am black and proud. I am not the candidate for the women's movement of this country, although I am a woman, and I am equally proud of that. . . . I am the candidate of the people."

With this announcement on January 25, 1972, Shirley Chisholm made political history. She was the first black woman to run for the presidential nomination of a major party. Who was Shirley Chisholm?

Shirley St. Hill was born in Brooklyn, New York, in 1924. From the age of three to nearly 10, she lived with her grandmother in Barbados. When she returned to her family in Brooklyn, she attended New York public schools. She received a degree in sociology from Brooklyn College. She met and married Conrad Chisholm.

In the early 1960s, Chisholm and others formed the Unity Democratic Club. Although unsupported by the males in the club, she ran for the New York State Assembly in 1964. She won, and two years later she was reelected. In 1968, she ran for Congress. She won the primary election and then beat her Republican opponent. She became the first black woman in the House of Representatives. She served seven terms.

In the 1970s, both the civil rights and the women's movements were asking, "Why not a woman president?" In 1972, Chisholm was urged to run. Although her primary election percentages were small, she stayed in the race to give America's neglected groups a choice. In the end, she was not the Democratic Party's nominee, but she had proven that a black woman could be a serious candidate.

Main Idea	1		
		Answer	**Score**
	Mark the *main idea*	M	15
	Mark the statement that is *too broad*	B	5
	Mark the statement that is *too narrow*	N	5
	a. Shirley Chisholm was active in politics.	☐	_____
	b. Shirley Chisholm was the first black woman to run for president.	☐	_____
	c. Shirley Chisholm lived for a time in Barbados.	☐	_____

Subject Matter   **2**   This passage deals mainly with
- [ ] a. the personal life of Shirley Chisholm.
- [ ] b. the political career of Shirley Chisholm.
- [ ] c. U.S. history in the 1970s.
- [ ] d. the history of presidential campaigns.

_____

Supporting Details   **3**   Shirley Chisholm was one of the founders of the
- [ ] a. Unity Democratic Club.
- [ ] b. New York State Assembly.
- [ ] c. women's movement.
- [ ] d. Republican Party.

_____

Conclusion   **4**   This passage leads the reader to believe that
- [ ] a. women politicians in the 1960s and 1970s were not unusual.
- [ ] b. Chisholm became president of the United States.
- [ ] c. Chisholm's presidential campaign was an important milestone in U.S. history.
- [ ] d. a women will never be president.

_____

Clarifying Devices   **5**   The basic pattern used to develop this passage is
- [ ] a. personal narrative.
- [ ] b. question and answer.
- [ ] c. comparison and contrast.
- [ ] d. chronological order.

_____

Vocabulary in Context   **6**   The word <u>nomination</u> means
- [ ] a. naming as a candidate for office.
- [ ] b. winner of a political race.
- [ ] c. fund-raiser.
- [ ] d. religious group.

_____

Add your scores for questions 1–6. Enter the total here and on the graph on page 159.   **Total Score**

_____

31 The Homeless

People without homes have always been present in America. In the past, they were called *hoboes, bums,* or *drifters.* These people received a new name in the early 1980s when activists named them *the homeless.*

The types of people who were homeless also changed in the 1980s. No longer were they primarily older men. They were younger, with an average age of 35. Their numbers consisted of women, children, adolescents, and entire families. They were of many races and cultures. No longer were they only in the inner city. They lived in rural areas and in large and small cities. No longer were they invisible to the people with homes and jobs. The homeless of the 1980s lived in packing crates and doorways. They slept on sidewalks and in public parks. They begged money from passersby and pushed their possessions in shopping carts.

Counting the numbers of homeless people is difficult. However, in 1984 the Department of Housing and Urban Development estimated the homeless population at between 250,000 and 350,000. In 1990 the Census Bureau counted about 459,000 people in shelters, in cheap hotels, and on the streets. In 1995 the National Alliance to End Homelessness estimated that there were 750,000 homeless Americans.

The homeless of the 1980s also began to speak out for themselves. Some spoke to Congress and to government committees controlling funding for social programs. Street newspapers, such as Chicago's *Streetwise* and Boston's *Spare Change,* had stories, poems, and essays that expressed the homeless viewpoint. The visible and vocal presence of the homeless prompted help from volunteers and government agencies. But what is still needed is a solution to the <u>plight</u> of America's homeless.

Main Idea	1		Answer	Score
	Mark the *main idea*		M	15
	Mark the statement that is *too broad*		B	5
	Mark the statement that is *too narrow*		N	5
	a. Homelessness is a real problem.		☐	___
	b. Homelessness in America changed in the 1980s.		☐	___
	c. Some homeless people live in packing crates.		☐	___

Score 15 points for each correct answer.　　　　　**Score**

Subject Matter　2　This passage is mainly about
　　　　　☐ a. the history of the homeless.
　　　　　☐ b. the homeless in the 1980s and 1990s.
　　　　　☐ c. one homeless person's story.
　　　　　☐ d. a way to provide homes for the homeless.　　____

Supporting Details　3　One way the homeless spoke out about their problem was by
　　　　　☐ a. writing books.
　　　　　☐ b. expressing their viewpoints in street newspapers.
　　　　　☐ c. moving to rural areas.
　　　　　☐ d. being elected to government office.　　____

Conclusion　4　Homelessness in the 1980s was
　　　　　☐ a. less of a problem than in earlier years.
　　　　　☐ b. a problem mostly of older men.
　　　　　☐ c. more widespread than earlier.
　　　　　☐ d. easier to count with each passing year.　　____

Clarifying Devices　5　The size of the homeless population is indicated through
　　　　　☐ a. agency statistics.
　　　　　☐ b. adjectives such as "many" and "few."
　　　　　☐ c. a graph.
　　　　　☐ d. a quoted expert.　　____

Vocabulary in Context　6　The word plight means
　　　　　☐ a. hopelessness.
　　　　　☐ b. fight.
　　　　　☐ c. distressing situation.
　　　　　☐ d. lack of money.　　____

Add your scores for questions 1–6. Enter the total here　　**Total**
and on the graph on page 159.　　**Score**　　____

63

32 The Sahara

The name *Sahara* derives from the Arabic word for "desert" or "steppe." At 3.5 million square miles, an area roughly the size of the United States, the Sahara in northern Africa is the largest desert in the world. It spans the continent from the Atlantic Ocean to the Red Sea. Daytime temperatures can reach as high as 130°F. The humidity sometimes gets into the teens. But it can also be as low as 2.5 percent, the lowest in the world. Most of the Sahara receives less than five inches of rain per year, while large areas sometimes have no rainfall at all for years.

At the heart of the Sahara is the landlocked north African country of Niger. Here the sand dunes can be 100 feet tall and several miles long. Here sand plains stretch over an area larger than Germany where there is neither water nor towns. Yet sitting in the midst of the surrounding desert is the town of Bilma. Suddenly there are pools of clear water. Surprisingly, there are groves of date palms. Underground water resources, or oases, sufficient to support irrigated agriculture are found in dry stream beds and depressions. Irrigation ditches run off a creek to water fields. Corn, cassava, tea, peanuts, hot peppers, and orange, lime, and grapefruit trees grow in these fields. Donkeys and goats graze on green grass.

The Sahara of Niger is still a region where you can see a camel <u>caravan</u> of 500 camels tied together in loose lines as long as a mile, traveling toward such oasis towns. There a caravan will collect life-sustaining salt, which is mined from watery basins, and transport it to settlements on the edge of the desert that are as much as 400 miles away. The round trip across the vast sands takes one month.

Main Idea	1		
		Answer	**Score**
	Mark the *main idea*	M	15
	Mark the statement that is *too broad*	B	5
	Mark the statement that is *too narrow*	N	5
	a. Africa has desert lands.	☐	____
	b. The Sahara is a large, forbidding African desert.	☐	____
	c. Lines of camels still cross the Sahara through Niger.	☐	____

Subject Matter   **2**   This passage is mostly about
- ☐ a. life in the Sahara.
- ☐ b. the deserts of Africa.
- ☐ c. Bilma.
- ☐ d. how camels travel in the desert.   ___

Supporting Details   **3**   Rainfall in most of the Sahara is
- ☐ a. less than five inches per year.
- ☐ b. less than ten inches per year.
- ☐ c. less than twenty inches per year.
- ☐ d. zero.   ___

Conclusion   **4**   The Sahara can be described as
- ☐ a. a place of contrasts.
- ☐ b. a place where no one lives.
- ☐ c. an area where the winters are cold.
- ☐ d. an area that appeals to many tourists.   ___

Clarifying Devices   **5**   The phrase "an area roughly the size of the United States" gives an indication of the size of
- ☐ a. northern Africa.
- ☐ b. Niger.
- ☐ c. the Sahara.
- ☐ d. all of Africa.   ___

Vocabulary in Context   **6**   In this passage, <u>caravan</u> means
- ☐ a. traveling circus.
- ☐ b. group traveling together through difficult country.
- ☐ c. railroad train.
- ☐ d. a small, fast sailing ship.   ___

Add your scores for questions 1–6. Enter the total here and on the graph on page 159.   **Total Score**   ___

33 The Highest Court

There is a <u>motto</u> carved over the entrance to the U.S. Supreme Court Building in Washington, D.C. The words are "Equal Justice Under Law." Supreme Court justices are dedicated to this motto.

The writers of the 1787 Constitution of the United States provided for a Supreme Court in Article III. Surprisingly, the Constitution does not specify the number of justices. Nor does it tell what their duties are. It also does not say when or where they are to meet.

In its early history, the Supreme Court had a relatively weak role in government. Its job was to interpret the Constitution. At that time, there weren't many interpretations to be made. As the United States grew, the Constitution was more often challenged. The Supreme Court responded to those challenges. Its strong responses helped to keep the Constitution up to date. They also strengthened the power of the court. It became a highly respected and equal third branch of government.

Today's court is made up of a chief justice and eight associate justices. All justices are appointed by the president. The appointments must be confirmed by the Senate. These are lifetime appointments. Lifetime appointments ensure that a justice's decisions do not affect his or her position in office. A justice can make decisions without fear of being fired, voted out of office, or replaced on political whim. On the other hand, lifetime appointments can be a problem. An aging justice's questionable health may hinder his or her ability to do the job. It is interesting to note that few justices have ever stepped down. Usually it is death rather than retirement that removes a justice from the Supreme Court bench.

Main Idea	1	Answer	Score
Mark the *main idea*		M	15
Mark the statement that is *too broad*		B	5
Mark the statement that is *too narrow*		N	5

a. Supreme Court justices have lifetime appointments. ☐ _____

b. The Supreme Court has become an important part of the U.S. government. ☐ _____

c. The Constitution calls for a Supreme Court. ☐ _____

Subject Matter   **2**   The content of this passage deals mainly with
- [ ] a. how to get appointed to the Supreme Court.
- [ ] b. the cases of the Supreme Court.
- [ ] c. a brief explanation of the Supreme Court.
- [ ] d. the phrase "Equal Justice Under Law."   _____

Supporting Details   **3**   Supreme Court justices are
- [ ] a. appointed by the president and confirmed by the Senate.
- [ ] b. voted into office by popular election.
- [ ] c. appointed by the president.
- [ ] d. chosen by the writers of the Constitution.   _____

Conclusion   **4**   The Supreme Court concerns itself with
- [ ] a. writing the Constitution.
- [ ] b. deciding whether laws are allowed by the Constitution.
- [ ] c. making laws.
- [ ] d. advising the president.   _____

Clarifying Devices   **5**   The information in the final paragraph
- [ ] a. gives information in narrative form.
- [ ] b. presents two sides of an issue.
- [ ] c. uses chronological order.
- [ ] d. tries to persuade the reader.   _____

Vocabulary in Context   **6**   The word <u>motto</u> means
- [ ] a. a phrase adopted as a rule.
- [ ] b. an address.
- [ ] c. a title.
- [ ] d. a decorative picture.   _____

Add your scores for questions 1–6. Enter the total here and on the graph on page 159.   **Total Score**   _____

34 The British in India

Around A.D. 1500, European traders began arriving in India. They wanted to take India's spices, rice, silk, and sugar cane back to Europe. The most successful trading company was the British East India Company, which was founded in 1600. With the help of the British government, this company gained great control over India.

British rule had some benefits for India. Important crops—including tea, coffee, and indigo—were introduced into India, and a national railroad system was built to help export goods. English was used across the many regions of India, providing one common language for the people.

But the British caused hardships too. For example, farmers in the Bengal region were forced to grow the export crop of indigo, used to make blue dye, instead of food. As a result, in 1770 about 10 million people died of famine. Britain also caused hardship in the Indian cloth industry by putting a 30 percent import tax on Indian cloth. This made Indian cloth too expensive to sell in Britain. When the Indians lost their British customers, their cloth industry was ruined. Then British cloth factories profited by selling British cloth to the Indians.

The Indian people were discontent under British rule. In 1930 Mohandas Gandhi took up the cause of Indian independence. He encouraged Indians to protest in nonviolent ways. He encouraged them not to pay taxes to the British, and he advocated a <u>boycott</u> of British-made products. After great struggle, both non-violent and violent, the British withdrew, and in 1947 India became a self-governing, independent country.

Main Idea   1

	Answer	Score
Mark the *main idea*	M	15
Mark the statement that is *too broad*	B	5
Mark the statement that is *too narrow*	N	5

a. The British ruled India.	☐	___
b. Mohandas Gandhi took up the cause of Indian independence in 1930.	☐	___
c. British rule of India had benefits and hardships.	☐	___

Subject Matter 2 This passage is mainly about
☐ a. the history of India.
☐ b. Britain's role in the history of India.
☐ c. the export crop of indigo.
☐ d. India's struggle for independence. _____

Supporting Details 3 A benefit of British rule was
☐ a. famine.
☐ b. decline of India's cloth industry.
☐ c. an independent Indian government.
☐ d. a national railroad system. _____

Conclusion 4 The Indian people were discontent because they did not
☐ a. like British cloth.
☐ b. like British taxes or British rule.
☐ c. want to speak English.
☐ d. want to be farmers. _____

Clarifying Devices 5 Benefits and hardships of British rule are contrasted in paragraphs
☐ a. 2 and 3.
☐ b. 1 and 2.
☐ c. 1 and 4.
☐ d. 3 and 4. _____

Vocabulary in Context 6 The word boycott means to
☐ a. buy a great deal of.
☐ b. allow only men and boys to use.
☐ c. refuse to buy, sell, or use.
☐ d. advertise. _____

Add your scores for questions 1–6. Enter the total here and on the graph on page 159. **Total Score** _____

35 Cargo Cults

The term *cargo cult* is used by anthropologists to describe South Pacific island religious movements that began in the 1860s. Island natives saw the economic <u>disparity</u> between themselves and white colonialists. Surely, they reasoned, the white men's ships being unloaded each day were the source of the white man's power. If the islanders could copy the arrival of cargo ships exactly, they would please their ancestral gods. Then they too would receive the same wealth.

World War II brought U.S. military troops to the islands of the South Pacific. The islanders had scarcely seen a piece of steel, let alone huge ships, airplanes, Jeeps, radios, refrigerators, and mobile hospitals. They were impressed and confused. The goods simply appeared. It could only be explained by magic. Again, as islanders did in the 19th century, the 20th century islanders reasoned that if the white man's magic was copied accurately, the islanders' cargo would come.

Cult rituals developed that often included preparations to receive the cargo. Airstrips were hacked out of the jungle; lookouts were posted to watch for airplanes; wooden radios were built with vines running out the back as antennae. Cult members dressed in makeshift U.S. Army uniforms and held military drills using bamboo "rifles." Military radio commands such as "Roger, out" and "You have landing clearance" were preserved as an oral tradition and passed down through the generations.

Not surprisingly, the results were disappointing. The planes and ships did not return. The cargo of the white man's world did not come to the islanders. Today cargo cultism in the Pacific islands is rare.

Main Idea	1		
		Answer	Score
Mark the *main idea*		M	15
Mark the statement that is *too broad*		B	5
Mark the statement that is *too narrow*		N	5

a. Cargo cults try to duplicate military uniforms and drills. ☐ _____

b. Cargo cults are a result of South Pacific islanders' exposure to material goods. ☐ _____

c. An unusual religion was practiced in the South Pacific Islands. ☐ _____

Score 15 points for each correct answer. **Score**

Subject Matter 2 This passage deals mainly with
- ☐ a. the work of South Pacific islanders.
- ☐ b. islanders' reaction to modern society's wealth.
- ☐ c. colonialism in the South Pacific.
- ☐ d. World War II in the South Pacific. _____

Supporting Details 3 In this passage, uniforms, drills, bamboo rifles, and radio commands are examples of
- ☐ a. 19th century colonialism.
- ☐ b. military training in the South Pacific.
- ☐ c. U.S. military troop activity.
- ☐ d. islanders' attempts to copy the white man's magic. _____

Conclusion 4 Cargo cults may be described as
- ☐ a. a result of the white man's greed.
- ☐ b. an unusual effect when two cultures meet.
- ☐ c. a good way for islanders to make money.
- ☐ d. illegal but often practiced. _____

Clarifying Devices 5 The quotation marks around the word *rifles* in the third paragraph shows that
- ☐ a. this is an important word in this passage.
- ☐ b. the items being discussed aren't really rifles.
- ☐ c. the word is quoted from someone's speech.
- ☐ d. this is a title of a short story. _____

Vocabulary in Context 6 The word <u>disparity</u> means
- ☐ a. lack of organization.
- ☐ b. difference.
- ☐ c. two or double of something.
- ☐ d. unhappiness. _____

Add your scores for questions 1–6. Enter the total here and on the graph on page 159. **Total Score** _____

36 Xi'an Warriors

In the city of Xi'an in central China lies one of archaeology's most astonishing discoveries. Two thousand years ago, the strong and powerful emperor Qin Shihuangdi died and was buried. What a burial it must have been! The gravesite is guarded by more than 8,000 life-size soldiers and horses made of clay. The figures are arranged in great military formations. They wear brightly painted military uniforms. They are lifelike in their postures and facial expressions. The figures are known as the Terra Cotta Warriors.

The site, discovered in 1974, is just 23 miles east of the ancient city of Xi'an. Three areas were <u>unearthed</u>. They are named Pit Number 1, Pit Number 2, and Pit Number 3. Pit Number 1 holds a huge rectangular military formation. There are about 6,000 terra cotta figures, horses, and chariots. The formation includes infantrymen and chariot soldiers. They stand in rows as vanguard, rearguard, and right and left flanks of a strong army. Pit Number 2 contains a battle formation of more than 1,400 terra cotta figures and horses. There are crossbowmen, charioteers, and cavalrymen. Pit Number 3 is divided into three sections. It includes an area with chariots and horses. There are only 64 armored warriors in this pit. It is thought that this pit represents the command headquarters of the emperor's army.

The discovery of the huge burial pits was an important find. It has provided an opportunity for archaeologists and historians to study the culture of Qin Shihuangdi. Qin Shihuangdi was clearly a powerful ruler. But could he have imagined his power reaching so far beyond his time?

Main Idea   1

	Answer	Score
Mark the *main idea*	M	15
Mark the statement that is *too broad*	B	5
Mark the statement that is *too narrow*	N	5

a. Qin Shihuangdi's burial site is an amazing archaeological find. ☐ _____

b. The three pits contain terra cotta figures. ☐ _____

c. Chinese archaeological sites are valuable. ☐ _____

Score 15 points for each correct answer.   **Score**

Subject Matter   **2**   The passage mainly describes
- [ ] a. the life and times of Qin Shihuangdi.
- [ ] b. the chariots.
- [ ] c. the contents of the burial pits.
- [ ] d. the facial expressions of the warriors.

    _____

Supporting   **3**   All three pits contained
Details
- [ ] a. crossbowmen.
- [ ] b. cavalrymen.
- [ ] c. Qin Shihuangdi.
- [ ] d. horses.

    _____

Conclusion   **4**   Qin Shihuangdi's power reaches beyond his time because
- [ ] a. he is still emperor.
- [ ] b. his burial pit provides information about his life and the era.
- [ ] c. he ruled a large portion of China.
- [ ] d. he was emperor for a very long time.

    _____

Clarifying   **5**   The question at the end suggests that the reader
Devices   should
- [ ] a. visit this site.
- [ ] b. consider the historical and archaeological importance of the site today.
- [ ] c. imagine the extent of Qin Shihuangdi's influence on modern warfare.
- [ ] d. investigate careers in archaeology.

    _____

Vocabulary   **6**   The word <u>unearthed</u> means
in Context
- [ ] a. dug up.
- [ ] b. reburied.
- [ ] c. covered with mud.
- [ ] d. sent into space.

    _____

Add your scores for questions 1–6. Enter the total here   **Total**
and on the graph on page 159.   **Score**   _____

37 Thirteen Days in October

John F. Kennedy, President of the United States, peered at the photographs taken by a U-2 spy plane flying high over Cuba. Nikita Khrushchev, premier of the Soviet Union, was installing offensive nuclear weapons just 90 miles off the Florida coast. It was October 15, 1962.

Kennedy called his advisers together. Some favored an immediate air strike and an invasion of Cuba; some thought the United States should put up a naval blockade around Cuba to turn away Soviet ships carrying weapons. Finally Kennedy decided. The navy would put up a blockade.

Khrushchev issued two orders. The Soviets would speed up work on the nuclear missile bases, and Soviet ship captains would ignore the blockade. Then the first unexpected event took place. Soviet ships approaching the blockade stopped dead in the water. The Soviet special envoy to Cuba had overruled Khrushchev and ordered Soviet ships to stop. Then on October 26, Kennedy received a letter from Khrushchev <u>proposing</u> that the Soviets would remove the missiles in exchange for a U.S. pledge never to invade Cuba. Before Kennedy could reply, a second Khrushchev letter arrived proposing a different solution. Khrushchev wanted U.S. missiles in Turkey removed in exchange for the removal of the Cuban missiles.

From the U.S. point of view, this was unacceptable, but Kennedy had one more strategy in mind. The terms of Khrushchev's first letter were acceptable, but not the terms of the second. So Kennedy ignored the second letter. He answered the first letter instead. He replied on October 27th, and the next day a message came from Khrushchev. Yes, the Soviet Union would accept the terms as stated in the president's letter. Somehow during those 13 days in October 1962, a war was avoided.

Main Idea	1	Answer	Score
	Mark the *main idea*	M	15
	Mark the statement that is *too broad*	B	5
	Mark the statement that is *too narrow*	N	5
	a. Communication is important.	☐	_____
	b. War between the Soviet Union and the United States was narrowly avoided in October 1962.	☐	_____
	c. The U.S. navy blockaded Soviet ships.	☐	_____

Score 15 points for each correct answer.   **Score**

Subject Matter   **2**   This passage is mostly about
☐ a. how Khrushchev became the Soviet premier.
☐ b. the naval blockade of Cuba.
☐ c. what Kennedy's advisers recommended.
☐ d. how the United States and the Soviet Union
avoided war in 1962.   _____

Supporting   **3**   The most important people affecting the outcome
Details   of the event in this passage are
☐ a. the Soviet special envoy and Khrushchev.
☐ b. Khrushchev and Kennedy.
☐ c. Kennedy's advisers.
☐ d. Kennedy and the Soviet ship captains.   _____

Conclusion   **4**   According to this passage, the main reason war
was avoided was the
☐ a. blockade.
☐ b. advisers.
☐ c. letters.
☐ d. U-2 spy plane.   _____

Clarifying   **5**   The first paragraph of this passage
Devices
☐ a. establishes the who, when, and where of
the incident.
☐ b. gives a brief history of U.S.-Soviet relations.
☐ c. moves from present time to past time.
☐ d. helps us understand Kennedy's character.   _____

Vocabulary   **6**   In this passage, <u>proposing</u> means
in Context
☐ a. putting forth for discussion.
☐ b. pretending.
☐ c. making an offer of marriage.
☐ d. bringing before a court of law.   _____

Add your scores for questions 1–6. Enter the total here   **Total**
and on the graph on page 159.   **Score**   _____

38 The Bones Tell Another Story

One field of applied anthropology is known as forensic anthropology. It specializes in the identification of human skeletal remains for legal purposes. Clyde C. Snow, forensic anthropologist, usually uses his science to identify victims of disasters and violent crimes. But sometimes Snow is asked to apply his skills to unusual cases.

In Montana, just west of the Black Hills of South Dakota, lies the Custer Battlefield. This is the location where the Battle of the Little Bighorn was fought on June 25, 1876. General George Custer and all his men died there, leaving no one to tell the U.S. cavalry's side of the story. That story could only be pieced together from evidence found at the site. When a brushfire burned off the prairie grass in 1983, previously undiscovered artifacts were uncovered. Among these were bones of Custer's soldiers, including one nearly intact skeleton. Archaeologists from the National Park Service asked Snow to examine these bones.

When the skeleton's bones were reassembled, they fit the description of only one of Custer's 267 men. That man was Mitch Boyer, one of Custer's scouts. One telling clue culled from Snow's investigation came from the skull's teeth. The arched marks on the left incisor and canine were the marks of a pipe smoker, and Boyer was a pipe smoker. The marks came from his habit of clenching the pipe stem between his teeth.

Indians who had fought in the battle had said that Boyer's detachment of troops was killed at another location. This location was a long way from where Boyer's bones were found. But forensic anthropology had now established a different scenario. Snow's identification of Boyer meant that a part of U.S. history had to be rewritten.

Main Idea   1

	Answer	Score
Mark the *main idea*	M	15
Mark the statement that is *too broad*	B	5
Mark the statement that is *too narrow*	N	5

a. Forensic anthropology helped to rewrite a piece of U.S. history. ☐ _____

b. Clyde Snow studied the bones found at the Little Bighorn battle site. ☐ _____

c. Forensic anthropology is a field of applied anthropology. ☐ _____

Score 15 points for each correct answer.   **Score**

Subject Matter   2   This passage deals mainly with the work of
- [ ] a. an archaeologist.
- [ ] b. a U.S. cavalry soldier.
- [ ] c. a National Park ranger.
- [ ] d. a forensic anthropologist.   _____

Supporting Details   3   The bones were not found until 1983 when
- [ ] a. the area of the battle was identified.
- [ ] b. a prairie fire burned away brush and uncovered hidden artifacts.
- [ ] c. people were celebrating the anniversary of the battle.
- [ ] d. an earthquake made the bones visible.   _____

Conclusion   4   The fact that Mitch Boyer's name was known suggests that
- [ ] a. this battle had been carefully studied.
- [ ] b. he rather than Custer had led the cavalry.
- [ ] c. the Indians thought he was the bravest white man.
- [ ] d. "Boyer" was a common last name in 1876.   _____

Clarifying Devices   5   The writer presents information in this passage by
- [ ] a. describing the battle.
- [ ] b. telling a story.
- [ ] c. proving that Custer had not been killed.
- [ ] d. presenting a series of questions and answers.   _____

Vocabulary in Context   6   The word culled means
- [ ] a. killed.
- [ ] b. selected.
- [ ] c. overlooked.
- [ ] d. thrown away.   _____

Add your scores for questions 1–6. Enter the total here and on the graph on page 159.   **Total Score**   _____

39 Port Chicago

On July 17, 1944, two munitions ships blew up at Port Chicago, 30 miles northeast of San Francisco, while being loaded with bombs, shells, and depth charges. Those on the pier and aboard the ships were instantly killed, leaving 320 men dead and 390 military personnel and civilians injured. It was the biggest disaster of World War II to take place in the United States. But the disaster had another disturbing figure: of the 320 men who died, 202 were African Americans. All the sailors performing the dangerous job of loading munitions were black.

A navy court of <u>inquiry</u> investigated the accident and placed no blame, saying "rough handling [of munitions] by an individual or individuals" may have been the cause. Traumatized by the explosion, 258 black loaders refused to return to work. They were imprisoned by the navy for three days. Most of those men, except for 50 seamen, then returned to work. These 50 were court-martialed, convicted of mutiny, and imprisoned until the end of the war. A young lawyer named Thurgood Marshall was outraged. "This is not 50 men on trial for mutiny," Marshall said. "This is the navy on trial for its whole vicious policy towards Negroes. Negroes in the navy don't mind loading ammunition. They just want to know why they are the only ones doing the loading!"

After the war, with Thurgood Marshall's persistence, the sentences of the 50 black sailors were reduced, but not overturned. However, the actions of the black sailors did make a difference. Soon after, white sailors were put to work side by side with black sailors loading ammunition at Port Chicago. Later, the navy followed through on a desegregation policy. And in 1967, the outspoken Thurgood Marshall became the first African-American justice of the U.S. Supreme Court.

Main Idea	1		
		Answer	**Score**
	Mark the _main idea_	M	15
	Mark the statement that is _too broad_	B	5
	Mark the statement that is _too narrow_	N	5

a. A disaster prompted changes in the navy's segregation policy. ☐ _____

b. Naval disasters were part of World War II. ☐ _____

c. Black sailors loaded ammunition at Port Chicago. ☐ _____

Subject Matter 2 This passage deals mainly with
☐ a. the battlefields of World War II.
☐ b. an injustice against black sailors.
☐ c. the life of Thurgood Marshall.
☐ d. how the two ships exploded. _____

Supporting Details 3 The 50 seamen were found guilty of
☐ a. conspiracy.
☐ b. talking to Thurgood Marshall.
☐ c. being absent without leave.
☐ d. mutiny. _____

Conclusion 4 Words like *disturbing* in the first paragraph and *made a difference* in the third paragraph suggest that the writer
☐ a. is critical of the sailors.
☐ b. sympathizes with the sailors.
☐ c. has no opinion about the incident.
☐ d. does not choose words very carefully. _____

Clarifying Devices 5 The information in this passage is presented
☐ a. through a fictitious story.
☐ b. starting in the present and going back into the past.
☐ c. in chronological order.
☐ d. through a series of descriptions. _____

Vocabulary in Context 6 In this passage, <u>inquiry</u> means
☐ a. a search for information and truth.
☐ b. curiosity.
☐ c. a question.
☐ d. an accident. _____

Add your scores for questions 1–6. Enter the total here and on the graph on page 159. **Total Score** _____

40 The Global Positioning System

In 1983 a Korean Airlines flight that had gone off course over the Soviet Union was shot down. All passengers, including several Americans, were killed. An investigation revealed that the pilots had set their starting point wrong, and the error was magnified as they flew. Today's technology ensures that this disaster could not happen again. That technology is the Global Positioning System (GPS), which is now used routinely for navigation on over-water flights. GPS is a great aid when the geography of an area is uncertain. It would have kept the Korean plane on course.

GPS is the network of 24 satellites launched and maintained by the U.S. military. The satellites are in continuous orbit 12,000 miles above the earth. Using geometry, the satellite signals precisely pinpoint a location. GPS was first used by the military to locate troops and tanks. It can tell where a missile or aircraft is. It can also tell how to get a weapon to a target. There are even hand-held, battery-operated GPS units for use by individual soldiers. In 1995 a U.S. Air Force pilot was shot down by a missile over Bosnia. He used a hand-held unit to find his exact position and radioed that information to his rescuers before he could be captured by the enemy.

What began as a military application is now finding a rapidly growing civilian market. Fishermen at sea, hikers on <u>remote</u> trails, and even rental cars are equipped with GPS. It is also being used in an increasing number of fire trucks, police cars, and ambulances. GPS can be used by farmers, too, to accurately guide a tractor in the field. Researchers have successfully used GPS to guide vehicles in fog and at night and to guide driverless vehicles. Although its military use is vital, it is most likely that GPS will get its greatest application in the civilian world.

Main Idea	1		
		Answer	Score
Mark the *main idea*		M	15
Mark the statement that is *too broad*		B	5
Mark the statement that is *too narrow*		N	5

a. A Korean Airlines flight went off course over the Soviet Union. ☐ _____

b. GPS is part of today's technology. ☐ _____

c. GPS has both military and civilian uses. ☐ _____

Subject Matter   2   This passage deals mainly with
☐ a. geometry.
☐ b. military tactics during war.
☐ c. using the Global Positioning System.
☐ d. problems with commercial airlines.   _____

Supporting Details   3   The story of the pilot in Bosnia in the second paragraph is an example of a
☐ a. military application of GPS.
☐ b. a civilian application of GPS.
☐ c. missile technology.
☐ d. the superiority of the U.S. military.   _____

Conclusion Devices   4   GPS could help you most if you
☐ a. were trying to learn all the state capitals.
☐ b. bought a new car that featured computerized maps.
☐ c. already knew your latitude and longitude.
☐ d. had a car breakdown on a country road.   _____

Clarifying   5   This passage, begins with an example of
☐ a. an event that would have benefited from GPS.
☐ b. GPS technology in use.
☐ c. a war caused by technology.
☐ d. Soviet technology.   _____

Vocabulary in Context   6   In this passage, <u>remote</u> means
☐ a. able to be operated from a distance.
☐ b. isolated.
☐ c. crowded.
☐ d. unwilling to be friendly.   _____

Add your scores for questions 1–6. Enter the total here   **Total**
and on the graph on page 159.   **Score**   _____

41 An Independent Woman

In the Puritan settlement of Newtown, Massachusetts, across the river from Boston, Anne Hutchinson, age 45, wife and mother of 13 children, stood before Governor John Winthrop and the Great and General Court of Massachusetts. She was the first colonial woman who had dared to publicly challenge the authority of the church and state. It was November 1637.

Eight years before, Winthrop and his band of Puritans sailed to the New World to establish a society where everyone observed the will of God. Now he read the charges against Anne Hutchinson. She had led women in prayer, and she had analyzed the various strengths and weaknesses of the colony's ministers. The Puritans believed that no woman should teach. Certainly no woman should criticize a minister.

The court unanimously decided against Anne Hutchinson. She was excommunicated from the Puritan church and banished from the Bay Colony. She and her family left Massachusetts to settle in Rhode Island.

News came back to Winthrop that Hutchinson's next child had been born dead. He instructed the colony's ministers to make this the subject of their sermons. Congregations were told that the dead child had been born a monster and that this was a fitting punishment from God. In 1643 Anne Hutchinson was again the subject of Bay Colony sermons. She had been murdered by Indians. It was fitting, the ministers announced, that this be the final blow in Mistress Hutchinson's earthly punishment.

For years the story of Anne Hutchinson was held up as a lesson to any who might put their own personal wishes above the laws of Puritan society. For Anne Hutchinson, her rebellion against <u>restrictive</u> Puritan society had cost her everything.

Main Idea	1		Answer	Score
	Mark the *main idea*		M	15
	Mark the statement that is *too broad*		B	5
	Mark the statement that is *too narrow*		N	5

a.	Puritan society was unforgiving.	☐ ____
b.	Anne Hutchinson's story was the subject of Puritan sermons.	☐ ____
c.	Anne Hutchinson risked everything to speak her beliefs in colonial Massachusetts.	☐ ____

Subject Matter   **2**   Another good title for this passage would be
- [ ] a. Governor Winthrop and His Wife.
- [ ] b. The "Sins" of Anne Hutchinson.
- [ ] c. A Child Is Born Dead.
- [ ] d. Life in the 1600s.

_____

Supporting Details   **3**   Authority to banish Hutchinson was held by the
- [ ] a. male citizens in the region.
- [ ] b. ministers she was accused of criticizing.
- [ ] c. Great and General Court of Massachusetts.
- [ ] d. Bay Colony.

_____

Conclusion   **4**   The Puritans
- [ ] a. wanted religious freedom, but only for the views they agreed with.
- [ ] b. were tolerant of all churchgoers.
- [ ] c. wanted to settle in Rhode Island.
- [ ] d. were quick to forgive any wrongdoers.

_____

Clarifying Devices   **5**   Which sentence helps clarify the word _banished_?
- [ ] a. The court unanimously decided against Anne Hutchinson.
- [ ] b. She was excommunicated from the Puritan church.
- [ ] c. She and her family left Massachusetts to settle in Rhode Island.
- [ ] d. This was a fitting punishment from God.

_____

Vocabulary in Context   **6**   The word <u>restrictive</u> means
- [ ] a. early American.
- [ ] b. respectable.
- [ ] c. permissive.
- [ ] d. confining.

_____

Add your scores for questions 1–6. Enter the total here and on the graph on page 159.   **Total Score**

_____

42 Separate No More

The "separate but equal" law in the United States allowed segregation to flourish. The first test of this law was in 1892, when a black man named Homer Plessy boarded a train on the East Louisiana Railroad. Plessy took a seat in a white coach and refused to move. He was arrested and charged with <u>violating</u> the law of segregation on public transportation. Plessy's case, *Plessy* v. *Ferguson,* was appealed to the U.S. Supreme Court. (The *v.* designation in court cases is an abbreviation for the word *versus,* which means "against.") In May 1896, the Court ruled against Plessy and upheld the separate but equal law, in spite of its being a violation of the equal protection clause of the 14th Amendment of the U.S. Constitution.

The separate but equal laws continued to be upheld until they were again challenged in the early 1950s by Oliver Brown. Brown, a minister in Topeka, Kansas, sued the local school board for the right to permit his daughter, Linda, to attend an all-white elementary school. Linda had been denied admission because she was black. *Brown* v. *Board of Education of Topeka* was taken to the Supreme Court. This time, in May 1954, the Supreme Court struck down "separate but equal" as unconstitutional. The Court stated:

> School segregation by state law causes a feeling of inferiority in black children that inflicts damage to their hearts and minds that may never be undone. Public school segregation by state law, therefore, violates the equal protection clause of the Fourteenth Amendment. . . . The old Plessy "separate but equal" rule is herewith formally overruled.

The Court's unanimous opinion influenced future civil rights legislation and launched the civil rights movement of the 1960s.

Main Idea 1		
	Answer	**Score**
Mark the *main idea*	M	15
Mark the statement that is *too broad*	B	5
Mark the statement that is *too narrow*	N	5

a. "Separate but equal" laws were struck down by the Supreme Court. ☐ _____

b. Some laws are unconstitutional. ☐ _____

c. *Brown* v. *Board of Education* launched the Civil Rights movement. ☐ _____

Subject Matter   **2**   This passage deals mainly with
- [ ] a. important civil rights cases.
- [ ] b. the Constitution of the United States.
- [ ] c. public transportation in the United States.
- [ ] d. education in the United States.   _____

Supporting Details   **3**   *Brown* v. *Board of Education* was decided in
- [ ] a. 1892.
- [ ] b. May 1896.
- [ ] c. May 1954.
- [ ] d. the 1960s.   _____

Conclusion   **4**   Prior to the Brown decision, separate but equal under the law meant that Linda Brown could not
- [ ] a. ride on the Louisiana Railroad.
- [ ] b. go to school.
- [ ] c. attend an all-white school.
- [ ] d. attend a school board meeting.   _____

Clarifying Devices   **5**   The information within the parentheses in the first paragraph
- [ ] a. is the topic sentence of the paragraph.
- [ ] b. is the writer's conclusion.
- [ ] c. is quoted material.
- [ ] d. clarifies information in the previous sentence.   _____

Vocabulary in Context   **6**   In this passage, <u>violating</u> means
- [ ] a. stealing.
- [ ] b. breaking.
- [ ] c. upholding.
- [ ] d. harming.   _____

Add your scores for questions 1–6. Enter the total here and on the graph on page 159.   **Total Score**   _____

43 The Changing Middle Class

The United States perceives itself to be a middle-class nation. However, middle class is not a real designation, nor does it carry privileges. It is more of a perception, which probably was as true as it ever could be right after World War II. The economy was growing, more and more people owned their own homes, workers had solid contracts with the companies that employed them, and nearly everyone who wanted a higher education could have one. Successful people enjoyed upward social mobility. They may have started out poor, but they could become rich. Successful people also found that they had greater geographic mobility. In other words, they found themselves moving to and living in a variety of places.

The middle class <u>collectively</u> holds several values and principles. One common value is financial independence—people don't want to be economically dependent on others. In addition, middle-class morality embraces principles of individual responsibility, importance of family, obligations to others, and belief in something outside oneself.

But in the 1990s those in the middle class found that there was a price for success. A *U.S. News & World Report* survey in 1994 indicated that 75 percent of U.S. citizens believed that middle-class families could no longer make ends meet. Both spouses now worked, as did some of the children; long commutes became routine; the need for child care put strains on the family; and public schools were not as good as they once were. Members of the middle class were no longer financing their lifestyles through earnings but were using credit to stay afloat. The understanding of just what *middle class* meant was changing.

Main Idea	1		
		Answer	**Score**
	Mark the *main idea*	**M**	15
	Mark the statement that is *too broad*	**B**	5
	Mark the statement that is *too narrow*	**N**	5

a. Being middle class involves believing in individual responsibility.   ☐   _____

b. People categorize themselves into classes.   ☐   _____

c. The middle class is held together by values its members have in common.   ☐   _____

Subject Matter   **2**   The information in this passage deals with
- ☐ a. an individual.
- ☐ b. a social and economic group.
- ☐ c. a political organization.
- ☐ d. government.

                     _____

Supporting Details   **3**   A common middle class principle is that
- ☐ a. people should always have fun.
- ☐ b. children should be seen and not heard.
- ☐ c. debt is nothing to worry about.
- ☐ d. the family is very important.

                     _____

Conclusion   **4**   In the years after World War II, the middle class could be defined as
- ☐ a. overburdened and in debt.
- ☐ b. hard working and suspicious.
- ☐ c. prosperous and optimistic.
- ☐ d. young and foolish.

                     _____

Clarifying Devices   **5**   The phrase *in other words* in the first paragraph means that the following statement is
- ☐ a. an exception to the previous idea.
- ☐ b. a denial of the previous idea.
- ☐ c. a restatement of the previous idea.
- ☐ d. a contrasting idea.

                     _____

Vocabulary in Context   **6**   The word collectively means
- ☐ a. as a group.
- ☐ b. hesitatingly.
- ☐ c. unknowingly.
- ☐ d. weakly.

                     _____

Add your scores for questions 1–6. Enter the total here and on the graph on page 159.   **Total Score**   _____

44 The Seneca Falls Convention

In 1848 Seneca Falls was a rural town in a remote corner of upstate New York. One small notice in the local *Seneca County Courier* announced that public meetings would be held at the Wesleyan Chapel on the subject of women's rights. A few dozen people were expected to attend, but to the astonishment of the organizers, hundreds of women showed up.

Elizabeth Cady Stanton (1815–1902) had never before spoken in public; few women in America had. As Stanton began, however, she discovered that she was a natural-born speaker. "Resolved," she read from the *Declaration of Sentiments and Resolutions*, "that it is the duty of the women of this country to secure to themselves their sacred right to the elective franchise." As expected, there was opposition to the resolution, but to Stanton's great relief and joy, it passed. Elizabeth Cady Stanton learned that she was not the only one in America who believed women deserved the right to vote.

The public expressed outrage and disgust. Newspapers reacted as if the women had set out to tear down the nation. One paper accused them of trying to "upheave existing institutions and overturn all the social relations of life." The clergy was outraged too. The women were accused of <u>undermining</u> organized religion and blaspheming God.

But something had been set in motion. More women's rights meetings were held, and two years later the first National Women's Rights Convention was held in Wooster, Massachusetts. When women finally gained the right to vote in a national election, in 1920, only one woman who had attended the Seneca Falls convention was still alive to cast her vote—72 years after Elizabeth Cady Stanton's act of monumental daring.

Main Idea	1	Answer	Score
	Mark the *main idea*	M	15
	Mark the statement that is *too broad*	B	5
	Mark the statement that is *too narrow*	N	5

a. Elizabeth Cady Stanton was an effective public speaker. ☐ _____

b. Women met about their rights. ☐ _____

c. The Seneca Falls convention paved the way for women's right to vote. ☐ _____

Score 15 points for each correct answer.   **Score**

Subject Matter 2 The best newspaper headline about the event
in this passage would be
☐ a. Seneca Falls—Home to Conventions.
☐ b. Women Want the Right to Vote.
☐ c. Stanton Speaks to Women.
☐ d. Wesleyan Chapel Site of Meeting.   _____

Supporting Details 3 The resolution read by Elizabeth Cady Stanton
was part of the
☐ a. *Seneca County Courier.*
☐ b. *Declaration of Independence.*
☐ c. *Declaration of Sentiments and Resolutions.*
☐ d. *Seneca Falls Convention Report.*   _____

Conclusion 4 It seems likely that
☐ a. women easily won the right to vote.
☐ b. Elizabeth Cady Stanton made many
more public speeches.
☐ c. the majority of women at the convention
disapproved of Stanton.
☐ d. Stanton later voted in a national election.   _____

Clarifying Devices 5 In the third paragraph, the phrase *the public*
refers specifically to
☐ a. the women's husbands.
☐ b. newspaper writers and clergy.
☐ c. politicians and office-seekers.
☐ d. the voting public.   _____

Vocabulary in Context 6 Undermining means
☐ a. planting bombs beneath.
☐ b. dressing in a scandalous manner.
☐ c. showing strong support for.
☐ d. weakening or destroying.   _____

Add your scores for questions 1–6. Enter the total here **Total**
and on the graph on page 159. **Score**   _____

45 Brazil's Favelas

In recent years, more than six million people have migrated to Brazilian cities from the rural areas. Many people are looking for a better life. Because they have nowhere else to stay, people live in temporary shelters, often while they collect materials for building a house. Their settlements are called *favelas*. Many are in the hills surrounding cities.

Building temporary shelters is one thing, but providing the necessary urban infrastructure is another. Roads, water, electricity, sanitation, schools, and health clinics in the favelas are inadequate.

Andarai, one of the smaller, older favelas, may look well-kept and permanent, but it is crowded. Through the self-help community association's efforts, Andarai has electricity and other improvements. But as you move up the hill, conditions <u>deteriorate</u>. Some of the housing is about to collapse. Some children are kept locked inside while their mothers are at work. Open sewers run down gullies. The people are destroying the forest near the top of the hill to get wood for fuel and building materials. They know this increases the chance of flood and landslides, but they have no alternative.

Most favela residents want better houses, more electricity, cleaner water, and improved roads. They need day-care centers, preschool programs, a community center, and health clinics. They also want to participate in making decisions about the favela.

Many people do improve their property; others move to better areas. Self-help community associations organize to improve conditions. The successes of the community associations show that when people work together, progress is possible.

Main Idea	1		
		Answer	**Score**
	Mark the *main idea*	M	15
	Mark the statement that is *too broad*	B	5
	Mark the statement that is *too narrow*	N	5
	a. People in Andarai need improvements.	☐	___
	b. People have migrated to Brazil's cities.	☐	___
	c. Brazil's favelas may provide housing, but they lack infrastructure.	☐	___

Score 15 points for each correct answer.   **Score**

Subject Matter **2** This passage deals mostly with
- ☐ a. the history of the favelas.
- ☐ b. why Brazil is a poor country.
- ☐ c. life in the favelas.
- ☐ d. community organizations.   _____

Supporting Details **3** Destroying the hillside forests may lead to
- ☐ a. floods and landslides.
- ☐ b. jobs.
- ☐ c. a decrease in annual rainfall.
- ☐ d. a rise in population.   _____

Conclusion **4** You can conclude from this passage that many Brazilian cities are
- ☐ a. located near the ocean.
- ☐ b. beautiful.
- ☐ c. overcrowded.
- ☐ d. decreasing in population.   _____

Clarifying Devices **5** The writer discusses conditions in favelas through
- ☐ a. cause and effect.
- ☐ b. a specific example.
- ☐ c. a personal narrative.
- ☐ d. a list of reasons.   _____

Vocabulary in Context **6** The word <u>deteriorate</u> means
- ☐ a. have limits.
- ☐ b. improve.
- ☐ c. are steeper.
- ☐ d. become worse.   _____

Add your scores for questions 1–6. Enter the total here   **Total**
and on the graph on page 159.   **Score**   _____

46 "Don't Ride the Buses"

"We are asking every Negro to stay off the buses on Monday in protest of the arrest and trial. Don't ride the buses to work, to town, to school, or anywhere on Monday." Within 48 hours of the December 1955 arrest of Rosa Parks, 5,000 <u>leaflets</u> with this statement were distributed to black churches throughout Montgomery, Alabama. The leaflets told of Rosa Parks's arrest due to her refusal to move to the so-called "colored section" in the back of a public bus. A young pastor, the Reverend Martin Luther King Jr., was elected to lead the boycott.

On the first day, African Americans traveled by cars, taxis, horse-drawn carts, mules, bicycles, and foot. They did not ride the buses. Through the winter months, organized car pools of about 300 vehicles and black-owned taxi companies carried passengers to their destinations. Churches bought station wagons and ran taxi services. The bus company's losses mounted, but the owners refused to give in.

Meanwhile, lawyers representing the boycott leaders petitioned the federal court to declare Alabama's bus segregation laws unconstitutional—and won. Alabama appealed to the U.S. Supreme Court, but no one knew when the case would be settled.

But another legal battle was closer to resolution. In November 1956, Montgomery city leaders petitioned the state circuit court to outlaw the black car pools, claiming they were a business operating without city permission. Without the car pools, the boycott would be defeated. Martin Luther King Jr. was at the Montgomery County courthouse waiting for the car pool decision when he heard this news: the U.S. Supreme Court had declared Alabama's bus-segregation laws unconstitutional. After a year of boycotting, the estimated 50,000 African-American citizens of Montgomery had prevailed.

Main Idea	1	Answer	Score
	Mark the *main idea*	M	15
	Mark the statement that is *too broad*	B	5
	Mark the statement that is *too narrow*	N	5

a. Segregation was a problem in Montgomery. ☐ _____

b. Rosa Parks was arrested in late 1955. ☐ _____

c. The 1955 bus boycott helped end segregation in Montgomery. ☐ _____

Subject Matter   2   This passage is mostly about
- ☐ a. Rosa Parks's life.
- ☐ b. the people who rode buses in Montgomery.
- ☐ c. the end of bus segregation in Montgomery.
- ☐ d. Rev. Martin Luther King Jr.'s life.   _____

Supporting Details   3   City leaders claimed that the black car pools
- ☐ a. were operating without city permission.
- ☐ b. should be carrying white people.
- ☐ c. were no threat to the bus system.
- ☐ d. operated unsafe vehicles.   _____

Conclusion   4   The statement "African-American citizens of Montgomery had prevailed" suggests that
- ☐ a. the citizens' actions were misguided.
- ☐ b. the boycott was a failure.
- ☐ c. a civil rights lawyer began the boycott.
- ☐ d. the boycott was a success.   _____

Clarifying Devices   5   Which sentence clarifies the true reason why the city was against black car pools?
- ☐ a. Churches . . . ran taxi services.
- ☐ b. The car pools were a business operating without city permission.
- ☐ c. Without the car pools, the boycott would be defeated.
- ☐ d. The bus company's losses were mounting.   _____

Vocabulary in Context   6   In this passage, <u>leaflets</u> are
- ☐ a. small hymn books.
- ☐ b. parts of a tree.
- ☐ c. sheets of printed material.
- ☐ d. receipts.   _____

Add your scores for questions 1–6. Enter the total here and on the graph on page 159.   Total Score   _____

47 Antarctica: Is There Something There?

Is there anything to do in Antarctica, the earth's fifth-largest and southernmost continent? There is if you want to experience the coldest climate on the earth with the lowest temperature ever recorded (−126.9°F), where annual precipitation varies from two inches of snowfall in the interior to 40 inches on the coast. There is if you think that three-mile-thick ice, mountain peaks, sea-washed coastlines, and a frozen waterfall bigger than Niagara Falls are scenic. There is if you would be intrigued by a lake with a water temperature of 77°F underneath its 10-foot-thick ice cover. Would you enjoy a three-month-long summer day? Would you like to live with a summer population of only several thousand people? Would you prefer wintering with a few hundred scientists and support personnel in extreme conditions?

Antarctica is more than one and one-half times the size of the United States. It covers about 5,500,000 square miles and is surrounded by the Antarctic Ocean. Some 98 percent of the continent is covered with ice, but there are some 1,500 square miles of windswept bare ground in the Dry Valleys area. Here, where ice does not hide the secrets of the earth, there are exposed pale brown and black layers of rock and blue-green algae-covered hillsides.

Algae, fungi, and bacteria that are insensitive to repeated freezing and thawing live between grains of sandstone. Bacteria-eating nematodes (<u>microscopic</u> worms) in the Dry Valleys go into a dry, lifeless state called anhydrobiosis when no moisture is present. But just a little bit of moisture from snow or a melt causes the nematodes to emerge from their freeze-dried state. Do you still think there is nothing to do or experience in Antarctica?

Main Idea   1

	Answer	Score
Mark the *main idea*	M	15
Mark the statement that is *too broad*	B	5
Mark the statement that is *too narrow*	N	5

a. Antarctica has a frozen waterfall.	☐	____
b. Antarctica is a place to see.	☐	____
c. Antarctica is a varied and interesting continent.	☐	____

Subject Matter 2 This passage is mostly about
- ☐ a. sights and conditions of Antarctica.
- ☐ b. explorers of Antarctica.
- ☐ c. tours to Antarctica.
- ☐ d. animals of Antarctica.   _____

Supporting Details 3 Antarctica has
- ☐ a. trees.
- ☐ b. polar bears.
- ☐ c. no solid surfaces.
- ☐ d. a lake with a water temperature of 77°F.   _____

Conclusion 4 The question at the end of the passage is intended to make the reader
- ☐ a. think about the information in the passage.
- ☐ b. want to travel to Antarctica.
- ☐ c. conclude that there is nothing to see in Antarctica.
- ☐ d. write a response to the passage.   _____

Clarifying Devices 5 The phrase *more than one and one-half times the size of the United States* tells the size of the
- ☐ a. Dry Valleys.
- ☐ b. continent of Antarctica.
- ☐ c. Antarctic Ocean.
- ☐ d. population of Antarctica.   _____

Vocabulary in Context 6 <u>Microscopic</u> means
- ☐ a. looking like a microscope.
- ☐ b. very nearsighted.
- ☐ c. very tiny.
- ☐ d. slightly smaller than a telescope.   _____

Add your scores for questions 1–6. Enter the total here and on the graph on page 159.   **Total Score**   _____

48 Evacuation from Saigon

April 28, 1975. The South Vietnamese government surrendered, and the North Vietnamese army was about to invade the capital city of Saigon. Ever since the early 1960s, U.S. presidents Kennedy, Johnson, and Nixon had been dispatching military advisors and troops to fight for the noncommunist government of South Vietnam. But for all the millions of dollars committed and the thousands of lives lost, the U.S. military failed to prevent South Vietnam from falling to the forces of communism. As a result, any Vietnamese who had opposed the communists was in <u>grave</u> danger.

Nine-year-old Hoang Nhu Tran and his family were among the thousands of Vietnamese forced to flee their homeland. Hoang's father was a major in the South Vietnamese air force. The Trans drove to Tan Son Nhut airport, where refugees were being evacuated on U.S. transport planes. By the time the Trans arrived, however, heavy rocket fire from oncoming tanks made takeoffs impossible. The airport was closed. The Trans had one final hope as they made their way back into the city and headed for the main dock on the Saigon River. The U.S. Navy had cargo ships and amphibious landing craft to evacuate the refugees, but there were more refugees than the boats could handle. Thousands pushed frantically up against the high wire fence that ran along the dock. Hoang's family forced its way into the hysterical crowd, somehow getting to the gate, where their military credentials got them into a boat.

The landing craft lumbered down the Saigon River and out into the South China Sea as Hoang looked up at the rockets shooting across the sky. There was no turning back. The Tran family headed eastward, away from the fallen city, having no idea of what might lie ahead. They only knew that Vietnam was no longer their home.

Main Idea	1		
		Answer	**Score**
Mark the *main idea*		M	15
Mark the statement that is *too broad*		B	5
Mark the statement that is *too narrow*		N	5

a. The fall of Saigon forced the evacuation of thousands of refugees. ☐ _____

b. Refugees escaped Saigon by boat. ☐ _____

c. South Vietnam surrendered to North Vietnam. ☐ _____

Subject Matter   2   This passage looks mainly at
- [ ] a. military maneuvers in Vietnam.
- [ ] b. the aftermath of the Vietnam war.
- [ ] c. Vietnamese in the United States.
- [ ] d. causes of war in Vietnam.

_____

Supporting Details   3   The Tan Son Nhut airport was closed because
- [ ] a. it was overcrowded with refugees.
- [ ] b. there were tanks on the runways.
- [ ] c. the invading North Vietnamese were firing rockets at it.
- [ ] d. bad weather reduced visibility.

_____

Conclusion   4   The Tran family's main reason for leaving Saigon was that
- [ ] a. their home had been bombed.
- [ ] b. they were in danger because Hoang's father had opposed the communists.
- [ ] c. they wanted to live in the United States.
- [ ] d. a war-torn country was no place to raise a child.

_____

Clarifying Devices   5   Which phrase helps clarify the meaning of *Saigon* in the first sentence?
- [ ] a. the capital city
- [ ] b. flee their homeland
- [ ] c. about to invade
- [ ] d. the South Vietnamese government

_____

Vocabulary in Context   6   In this passage, the word <u>grave</u> means
- [ ] a. burial place.
- [ ] b. life-threatening.
- [ ] c. dignified.
- [ ] d. important.

_____

Add your scores for questions 1–6. Enter the total here and on the graph on page 159.   **Total Score**   _____

49 Resurrecting a Spanish Galleon

Pensacola Bay in the Gulf of Mexico was a landing site for Spanish colonists during the 16th century. Underwater archaeologists were looking for evidence of this fact when in October 1992 they discovered a mound of ballast stones lying on a sandbar. Months of exploration and artifact analysis between 1992 and 1995 led to the conclusion that the wreck was one of the larger vessels in a Spanish fleet led by Captain Tristán de Luna y Arellano.

In 1559 the Luna expedition of 11 ships—loaded with supplies, weapons, 540 soldiers, and 240 horses—left Veracruz, Mexico. It also included more than 1,000 colonists and servants. The expedition's mission was to establish a military colony in what is now the state of Florida. On August 15, the fleet anchored in Pensacola Bay. The colonists went ashore to build a town. On September 19, a hurricane sank eight of the vessels, <u>dooming</u> the young colony.

Evidence of the lives of the unfortunate colonists had been sealed beneath a thick layer of oyster, clam, and mussel shells for nearly 450 years. Archaeologists uncovered leather shoes, butchered animal bones, and a small carved piece of wood in the shape of a 16th-century Spanish galleon. The discovery of a large metal pitcher, copper cooking cauldron, and copper skillet told the archaeologists that they had located the ship's galley. Rat bones, remains of mice, and body parts of cockroaches were evidence of the animal life on board. But there was little evidence of cargo. This probably means that the colonists salvaged what they could after the hurricane.

The Spanish galleon is now listed on the National Register of Historic Places. It offers a historical look at Spanish sea migration.

Main Idea	1		Answer	Score
	Mark the *main idea*		M	15
	Mark the statement that is *too broad*		B	5
	Mark the statement that is *too narrow*		N	5

a. Underwater archaeologists uncovered a Spanish galleon. ☐ _____

b. The galleon is listed on the National Register of Historic Places. ☐ _____

c. A galleon gives a look at the lives of 16th-century Spanish colonists. ☐ _____

Score 15 points for each correct answer.   **Score**

Subject Matter   **2**   This passage is mainly about
- ☐ a. what the wreck showed about the Spanish colonists.
- ☐ b. early settlements around Pensacola.
- ☐ c. the work of underwater archaeologists.
- ☐ d. Captain Tristán de Luna y Arellano.

_____

Supporting Details   **.3**   Archaeologists knew they had found the ship's galley when they uncovered
- ☐ a. a leather shoe.
- ☐ b. a cooking cauldron and skillet.
- ☐ c. mussel shells.
- ☐ d. a map carved in wood.

_____

Conclusion   **4**   This passage suggests the idea that life for early colonists was
- ☐ a. easy.
- ☐ b. violent.
- ☐ c. social.
- ☐ d. uncertain.

_____

Clarifying Devices   **5**   The second paragraph mainly presents
- ☐ a. a personal narrative of the shipwreck.
- ☐ b. a description of the setting.
- ☐ c. events in chronological order.
- ☐ d. comparison and contrast.

_____

Vocabulary in Context   **6**   Dooming means
- ☐ a. sinking.
- ☐ b. constructing.
- ☐ c. causing a bad outcome.
- ☐ d. arguing to make a point.

_____

Add your scores for questions 1–6. Enter the total here and on the graph on page 159.   **Total Score**

_____

50 Who Planned This Park?

Frederick Law Olmsted (1822–1903), a Connecticut farm boy, saw his first public park in Liverpool, England, as he accompanied his brother on a walking tour. He was impressed by the park's winding paths, open fields, lakes, and bridges. Perhaps the most wondrous thing of all was that the park was open to everyone.

A movement beginning in 1840 to set aside park land on New York City's Manhattan Island successfully culminated in 1856 with the purchase of 840 acres of rocky and swampy land, bought with about $5 million in state funds. Olmsted's chance meeting with a project organizer led to his applying for the job of park superintendent. In 1857 Olmsted was appointed superintendent of the proposed park, and the clearing of the site began. But a park needs a plan, so the park commissioners offered a $2,000 prize for a winning design.

Calvert Vaux, a British architect, asked Olmsted to <u>collaborate</u> with him on a park design, and Olmsted agreed. Vaux saw the park as a work of art, while Olmsted saw the park as a place for people to escape the bustle and noise of the city. Together they devised a plan that would give city dwellers a tranquil green park and would also preserve and enhance the natural features of the land. The commissioners voted in favor of Vaux and Olmsted's plan, and in 1858 the two became the official designers of New York City's Central Park.

It took millions of cartloads of topsoil to build Central Park's gentle slopes, shady glens, and steep, rocky ravines. Five million trees and shrubs were planted, a water-supply system was laid, and bridges, arches, roads, and paths were constructed. The park officially opened in 1876, and today, well over a century later, people still escape the bustle and noise of the city in Olmsted and Vaux's great work of art.

Main Idea	1		
		Answer	**Score**
	Mark the *main idea*	M	15
	Mark the statement that is *too broad*	B	5
	Mark the statement that is *too narrow*	N	5

a. Olmstead and Vaux planned and designed Central Park. ☐ ____

b. Olmstead and Vaux built shady glens and rocky ravines. ☐ ____

c. New York City needed parks. ☐ ____

Subject Matter   2   This passage is mainly
- [ ] a. a biography of Frederick Law Olmsted.
- [ ] b. an engineering plan for Central Park.
- [ ] c. a history of the planning of Central Park.
- [ ] d. a guided walking tour of Central Park.   _____

Supporting Details   3   Olmsted became superintendent of Central Park because of
- [ ] a. a chance meeting with one of the park's organizers.
- [ ] b. his winning a design competition.
- [ ] c. his friendship with Calvert Vaux.
- [ ] d. his hard work in clearing the land.   _____

Conclusion   4   The phrase "great work of art" in the last sentence indicates that the writer thinks Central Park
- [ ] a. is only for people who can afford it.
- [ ] b. is a beautiful place.
- [ ] c. is like a museum.
- [ ] d. should be looked at but not touched.   _____

Clarifying Devices   5   The basic organization of this passage is
- [ ] a. personal narrative.
- [ ] b. from latest event to earliest.
- [ ] c. from earliest event to latest.
- [ ] d. comparison and contrast.   _____

Vocabulary in Context   6   The word <u>collaborate</u> means
- [ ] a. vote.
- [ ] b. comment.
- [ ] c. disagree.
- [ ] d. work together.   _____

Add your scores for questions 1–6. Enter the total here and on the graph on page 159.   **Total Score**   _____

51 Space Invaders

A normal conversation between strangers involves more than talk. It also involves the <u>dynamics</u> of space interaction. If one person gets too close, the other person will back up. If the first person invades the other's space again, the other person will back up again. The person who finds himself or herself backing up is trying to increase the distance of the comfort zone. The person closing in is trying to decrease that distance. Most likely neither person is fully aware of what is going on.

In the 1960s, American anthropologist Edward T. Hall was a pioneer in the study of human behavioral use of space. His field of study became known as *proxemics*. Hall said that personal space for people in the United States can be defined as having four distinct zones: the intimate zone within 18 inches of your body, for whispering and embracing; the personal zone of 18 inches to four feet, for talking with close friends; the social zone of four to 10 feet, for conversing with acquaintances; and the public zone of 10 to 25 feet, for interacting with strangers or talking to a group.

Historians say that our standards of personal space began with the Industrial Revolution in the 18th century. In cities such as London and New York, people of different social and economic classes were suddenly crammed together, so they unconsciously developed a commonly understood code of courtesy to restrict the space around them.

People exhibit nonverbal messages of discomfort when their zones are violated. Invaded people might tap their toes, pull at their hair, become completely rigid, or even become angry. As Hall noted in his landmark work, a comfortable conversation needs to include the parameters of human personal space.

Main Idea	1	Answer	Score
Mark the *main idea*		M	15
Mark the statement that is *too broad*		B	5
Mark the statement that is *too narrow*		N	5

a. People have a need for personal comfort zones.	☐	____
b. People exhibit nonverbal messages of discomfort.	☐	____
c. People engage in conversations.	☐	____

Subject Matter   **2**   This passage is mostly about
- [ ] a. what nonverbal communication is.
- [ ] b. human conversation.
- [ ] c. the life of Edward T. Hall.
- [ ] d. human behavioral use of space.   _____

Supporting Details   **3**   Edward T. Hall identified
- [ ] a. interactions between strangers.
- [ ] b. angry people.
- [ ] c. four zones of personal space.
- [ ] d. the Industrial Revolution.   _____

Conclusion   **4**   If you and a close friend began talking when you were eight feet apart, you would probably soon
- [ ] a. move closer together.
- [ ] b. move farther apart.
- [ ] c. begin talking more softly.
- [ ] d. ask another friend to join the conversation.   _____

Clarifying Devices   **5**   The third paragraph provides
- [ ] a. a historical perspective on personal space.
- [ ] b. an economic reason for personal space.
- [ ] c. an overview of Edward T. Hall's field of study.
- [ ] d. a definition of personal space.   _____

Vocabulary in Context   **6**   The word <u>dynamics</u> means
- [ ] a. difficulties.
- [ ] b. forces or influences that cause change.
- [ ] c. largeness.
- [ ] d. explosions so large they are beyond belief.   _____

Add your scores for questions 1–6. Enter the total here and on the graph on page 160.   **Total Score**   _____

52 City Planning

City planners are the people who guide the development of cities and towns. They advise local governments on ways to improve communities, and they design entirely new communities. In South Florida, for example, city planners are working to improve existing communities. The population of the area is expected to increase from 5.5 million to 7.5 million by 2020. This growth is headed to the west, where there is still open land. But western growth creates a costly need for new roads, and it is a threat to the ecological system of the Florida Everglades. City planners are trying to <u>lure</u> people back into the older, more developed eastern section of the region by funneling growth in that direction and away from the western section.

City planners also plan and develop new communities. These communities, called new cities or new towns, include both places to live and places to work. New cities, such as Brazil's capital Brasilia, a community founded in 1900, can be constructed far from existing cities. Such cities are designed with enough facilities and job opportunities for all their residents. Building completely new cities is very costly, however. Brasilia and Canberra, Australia, are two examples of the few new cities that have ever been completed.

New towns are different from new cities in that they are built within commuting distance of large cities. They may also be planned communities within a city. New towns provide jobs for many of their residents, but they also rely on neighboring cities for jobs. Two of the first new towns built in the United States were Columbia, Maryland, and Reston, Virginia. At the end of the 20th century, an estimated 100 new towns were planned or under construction in the United States.

Main Idea	1		
		Answer	**Score**
	Mark the *main idea*	M	15
	Mark the statement that is *too broad*	B	5
	Mark the statement that is *too narrow*	N	5

a. New communities include places to live and work. ☐ _____

b. City planners improve old communities or design new ones. ☐ _____

c. City planners are at work around the world. ☐ _____

Score 15 points for each correct answer.   **Score**

Subject Matter   **2**   This passage is mostly about
- ☐ a. choosing a good city planner.
- ☐ b. the planning of Reston, Virginia.
- ☐ c. the planning of Brasilia and Canberra.
- ☐ d. the work of city planners.   _____

Supporting Details   **3**   Brasilia, Brazil, is an example of
- ☐ a. an improved old city.
- ☐ b. a planned new city.
- ☐ c. a planned new town.
- ☐ d. a suburban development.   _____

Conclusion   **4**   You would most likely hire a city planner if you needed
- ☐ a. advice on which crops will grow best on your land.
- ☐ b. someone to plan a city election campaign.
- ☐ c. someone to design a new office building.
- ☐ d. someone to guide the development of a new suburb.   _____

Clarifying Devices   **5**   The number 2.0 million indicates the predicted
- ☐ a. decrease in South Florida's population.
- ☐ b. increase in South Florida's population.
- ☐ c. number of city planners in the year 2020.
- ☐ d. number of towns to be planned by 2050.   _____

Vocabulary in Context   **6**   In this passage, <u>lure</u> means
- ☐ a. an item to use while fishing.
- ☐ b. lie to.
- ☐ c. attract.
- ☐ d. perform magic on.   _____

Add your scores for questions 1–6. Enter the total here and on the graph on page 160.   **Total Score**   _____

53 Archaeological Fact or Fiction?

The demolition of a downtown Miami, Florida, apartment building in 1998 uncovered an archaeological site. The site contained many artifacts and a unique circle of holes cut into limestone bedrock. The 38-foot circle formed by the holes appeared to have an east–west axis that <u>aligned</u> with the rising and setting of the sun on the equinox. The formation became known as the Miami Circle. Archaeologist Robert Carr speculated that the circle and its holes once supported the wall posts of a structure. Perhaps the structure was a temple or council house constructed between 500 and 700 years ago. Or was it?

Thousands of genuine artifacts found at the site helped to support Carr's theory. The artifacts are typical of the Tequesta Indians, who lived in the area before the Spanish arrived in the 1500s. There were potsherds, stone axes, and beads. Also found were a five-foot shark and a sea turtle. The shark and the sea turtle were buried with their heads to the west and tails to the east.

Historical preservationists said the Miami Circle was the only "cut-in-rock prehistoric structural footprint ever found in eastern North America." However, others questioned its authenticity. This was because embedded in the limestone circle was a 1950s septic tank. Jerald T. Milanich, curator in archaeology of the Florida Museum of Natural History, wanted to know if Carr's "pre-Columbian postholes" were actually part of a 1950s septic drain field. Before he would believe that the septic tank and the circle are just a coincidence, as Carr believed, Milanich wanted more evidence. He called for radiocarbon dating, soil samples, and examination of the tool marks on the inside of the holes. Said Milanich, "When faced with coincidences and mysteries, an archaeologist needs to eliminate alternative explanations."

Main Idea	1	Answer	Score
	Mark the *main idea*	M	15
	Mark the statement that is *too broad*	B	5
	Mark the statement that is *too narrow*	N	5

a. An archaeological site found in Miami may not be genuine. ☐ _____

b. Archaeologists sometimes find unusual sites. ☐ _____

c. Potsherds seemed to suggest that Tequesta Indians had built the site. ☐ _____

Score 15 points for each correct answer. **Score**

Subject Matter 2 This passage is mostly about
- ☐ a. the lifestyle of the Tequesta Indians.
- ☐ b. why buildings should not be demolished in Miami.
- ☐ c. the authenticity of an archaeological site in Miami.
- ☐ d. how archaeological sites are excavated. _____

Supporting Details 3 The Tequesta Indians lived in the area
- ☐ a. before the 1500s.
- ☐ b. in the 1950s.
- ☐ c. after the 1990s.
- ☐ d. after the Spanish arrived. _____

Conclusion 4 The information in this passage is
- ☐ a. only factual.
- ☐ b. only speculative.
- ☐ c. both factual and speculative.
- ☐ d. only one person's opinion. _____

Clarifying Devices 5 Potsherds, stone axes, and beads are examples of
- ☐ a. luxury items.
- ☐ b. things found in the Caribbean.
- ☐ c. things found in the Miami River.
- ☐ d. artifacts found at the site. _____

Vocabulary in Context 6 The word <u>aligned</u> means
- ☐ a. became allies with.
- ☐ b. lined up with.
- ☐ c. strong.
- ☐ d. deeply carved into the earth. _____

Add your scores for questions 1–6. Enter the total here and on the graph on page 160. **Total Score** _____

54 A Deadly Game of Hide and Seek

For six years, Mexico had been locked in a bloody revolution, with each state controlled by a different <u>warlord</u>. U.S. citizens had more than a billion dollars invested in Mexican property and industry. So, to protect U.S. interests, the United States stepped in. President Woodrow Wilson, in hopes of stabilizing the Mexican government, supported Venustiano Carranza as the head of Mexico.

Francisco "Pancho" Villa, warlord of Northern Mexico, was outraged. The way Villa saw it, Wilson could not possibly have made a worse choice than Villa's rival, Carranza. In retaliation, Villa led his rebel army northward in 1916. His targets were his own Mexican government and the United States with its meddling president. Villa and his *Villistas* attacked the little border town of Columbus, New Mexico, to show Wilson and Carranza that they'd double-crossed the wrong man.

President Wilson ordered General John Pershing to cross the border into Mexico with some 6,600 cavalrymen. Their orders were to capture the bandit Villa dead or alive. All through the summer and fall of 1916, Pershing's forces wandered aimlessly through the Mexican state of Chihuahua, while Villa's army grew. Rumors reported that Villa's forces were as strong as 18,000 men.

When Pershing failed even to sight the elusive Villa, a joint Mexican-American Commission negotiated an agreement allowing both sides to back away peacefully. On February 5, 1917, the last members of the Pershing Expedition left Mexico for good. The cost to the United States: about 100 casualties and some $130 million spent in the pursuit of an outlaw whom U.S. troops could not bring to justice. But Villa did stop his raids on the U.S. side of the border.

Main Idea	1	Answer	Score
	Mark the *main idea*	M	15
	Mark the statement that is *too broad*	B	5
	Mark the statement that is *too narrow*	N	5

a. U.S. presidents have attempted to influence Mexican politics. ☐ _____

b. Pancho Villa led troops into the United States. ☐ _____

c. Pancho Villa attacked the United States in revenge for U.S. meddling. ☐ _____

Score 15 points for each correct answer.   **Score**

Subject Matter 2 Another good title for this passage would be
☐ a. A New President for Mexico.
☐ b. General Pershing Wins a Battle.
☐ c. Pancho Villa and the U.S. President.
☐ d. Famous Mexican Leaders.   _____

Supporting Details 3 As Pershing's troops wandered in Mexico,
☐ a. Pancho Villa was brought to justice.
☐ b. Pancho Villa's army decreased in number.
☐ c. Villa was killed by his own men.
☐ d. Pancho Villa's army increased in number.   _____

Conclusion 4 In dealing with Pancho Villa, the United States
☐ a. got nothing for all its efforts.
☐ b. was the clearcut winner.
☐ c. apparently did frighten Villa somewhat.
☐ d. agreed to name Villa leader of Mexico.   _____

Clarifying Devices 5 Information in this passage is generally presented
☐ a. from earliest to latest.
☐ b. in order of importance.
☐ c. in spatial order.
☐ d. from latest to earliest.   _____

Vocabulary in Context 6 The word <u>warlord</u> means a
☐ a. guardian.
☐ b. military ruler.
☐ c. follower.
☐ d. wizard.   _____

Add your scores for questions 1–6. Enter the total here and on the graph on page 160.   **Total Score**   _____

55 Can the Earth Feed Its People?

In 1950 the world population's reached almost 2.5 billion, and predictions were that by the year 2000 there would be more than 5 billion people. Some experts were convinced that the world was on the verge of widespread <u>famine</u>.

One reaction to the problem was the green revolution of the 1960s. This effort multiplied agricultural yields in poor countries by introducing new high-yield grains. India, for example, doubled its wheat crop in just six years. The food supply increased faster than demand, and the price of staple foods fell. One result of the green revolution was that global food production today remains sufficient to provide every person with an adequate diet. Yet the problem of hunger remains—about 20 percent of the developing world's population is undernourished.

The immediate cause of world hunger has less to do with food production than with food distribution. For example, millions of acres in Africa, Asia, and Latin America once supported subsistence farming. Now the lands are used to raise crops such as coffee, tea, chocolate, bananas, and beef for export. The subsistence farmers have been relocated to urban areas, where there is often no employment, or to areas unsuited for farming. Small farmers and poor countries did not benefit from the green revolution because they could not afford the expensive seeds and chemicals that make agriculture productive. Despite falling food prices, hundreds of millions of people cannot afford a balanced diet. It is estimated that in the United States alone 30 million people—mostly children, the elderly, and the working poor—are hungry. The answer to the question seems to be that yes, the world can provide enough food, but it is up to people to find a way to distribute the food so that everyone has an adequate food supply.

Main Idea	1	Answer	Score
	Mark the *main idea*	**M**	15
	Mark the statement that is *too broad*	**B**	5
	Mark the statement that is *too narrow*	**N**	5

a. The green revolution increased agricultural yields in poor countries. ☐ _____

b. Hunger is a world problem. ☐ _____

c. World food production has increased, but people are still hungry. ☐ _____

Subject Matter   **2**   This passage is mainly about
- ☐ a. the history of world hunger.
- ☐ b. world hunger in the 1950s and 1960s.
- ☐ c. one nation's story.
- ☐ d. problems of and solutions to world hunger.   _____

Supporting Details   **3**   The percentage of the developing world population that continues to be undernourished is
- ☐ a. 2.5 billion.
- ☐ b. 20 percent.
- ☐ c. 30 million.
- ☐ d. 6 percent.   _____

Conclusion   **4**   One reason for the early concern about worldwide hunger was
- ☐ a. the green revolution.
- ☐ b. rapid worldwide population growth.
- ☐ c. farmers unwilling to plant every year.
- ☐ d. people not wanting to eat healthful foods.   _____

Clarifying Devices   **5**   The third paragraph is mainly developed through
- ☐ a. examples.
- ☐ b. comparison and contrast.
- ☐ c. a persuasive argument.
- ☐ d. a description.   _____

Vocabulary in Context   **6**   The word <u>famine</u> means
- ☐ a. population explosion.
- ☐ b. excessive enthusiasm.
- ☐ c. danger.
- ☐ d. a lack of food.   _____

Add your scores for questions 1–6. Enter the total here and on the graph on page 160.   **Total Score**   _____

56 The Family

The structure of a family takes different forms in different places around the world and even in different groups within a society. The family's form changes as it adapts to changing social and economic influences. Until recently, the most common form in North America was the nuclear family, consisting of a married couple with their minor children. The nuclear family is an independent unit. It must be prepared to fend for itself. Individual family members strongly depend on one another. There is little help from outside the family in emergencies. Elderly relatives of a nuclear family are cared for only if it is possible for the family to do so. In North America, the elderly often do not live with the family; they live in retirement communities and nursing homes.

There are many parallels between the nuclear family in industrial societies and the families in societies that live in harsh environments, such as the Inuits. The nuclear family structure is well adapted to a life of <u>mobility</u>. In harsh conditions, mobility allows the family to hunt for food. For North Americans, the hunt for jobs and improved social status also requires mobility.

The nuclear family was not always the North American standard. In a more agrarian time, the small nuclear family was usually part of a larger extended family. This might have included grandparents, mother and father, brothers and sisters, uncles, aunts, and cousins. In North America today, there is a dramatic rise in the number of single-parent households. About two-thirds of all households in the United States are headed by divorced, separated, or never-married individuals. The structure of the family, not just in North America, but throughout the world, continues to change as it adapts to changing conditions.

Main Idea	1	Answer	Score
	Mark the *main idea*	M	15
	Mark the statement that is *too broad*	B	5
	Mark the statement that is *too narrow*	N	5

a. North American family forms are influenced by the conditions people live under. ☐ _____

b. The nuclear family form was once the most common in North America. ☐ _____

c. Families take different forms. ☐ _____

Subject Matter   **2**   Another good title for this passage would be
- ☐ a. What Makes a Family?
- ☐ b. The Life of the Inuits.
- ☐ c. Living with Hardship.
- ☐ d. The Failure of the Nuclear Family.   _____

Supporting Details   **3**   A nuclear family is defined as
- ☐ a. a married couple with their minor children.
- ☐ b. a single father with minor children.
- ☐ c. parents, grandparents, and children.
- ☐ d. parents, children, and aunts and uncles.   _____

Conclusion   **4**   The information in this passage would most likely be found in
- ☐ a. an anthropology textbook.
- ☐ b. a biology textbook.
- ☐ c. a mathematics textbook.
- ☐ d. a geography textbook.   _____

Clarifying Devices   **5**   The information in the first paragraph is presented mainly through
- ☐ a. listing statistics.
- ☐ b. telling a story.
- ☐ c. pointing out similarities.
- ☐ d. pointing out differences.   _____

Vocabulary in Context   **6**   The word <u>mobility</u> means
- ☐ a. money.
- ☐ b. readiness to move.
- ☐ c. organization.
- ☐ d. skill.   _____

Add your scores for questions 1–6. Enter the total here and on the graph on page 160.   **Total Score**   _____

57 Alexandria's Sunken City

By the mid-fifth century A.D., the royal palaces and buildings within the Great Harbor of Alexandria, Egypt, had been destroyed by earthquakes and tidal waves. Over time the harbor floor dropped more than 20 feet. The ruined buildings of the Great Harbor sank beneath the water. Today archaeologist-divers, architects, photographers, geologists, and Egyptologists piece together information about the city that lies on the floor of the harbor.

The water in the harbor is between 6 and 30 feet deep. This shallow depth allows archaeologists to use the latest technology to map the harbor's archaeological features. They use a plumb bob suspended from a buoy to trace the remains of streets and the outlines of fallen columns, capitals, statues, and stone blocks that litter the seabed of the modern harbor. The buoy, at the surface of the water, has two waterproof Global Positioning System (GPS) receivers. One receives signals from satellites passing overhead. The other receives signals from an onshore beacon. The GPS data is transmitted to two research vessels anchored in the harbor, where it is entered into a database. The database is used to <u>generate</u> a map of the location of the archaeological remains.

The mapping of Alexandria's eastern harbor was substantially completed in 1997. Then the archaeologist-divers began excavations. The architectural and sculptural pieces were cleaned, identified, drawn, and photographed. Each find was given an inventory number, and its height, orientation, and location were recorded. The work is not complete, but plans are being considered to someday create an underwater archaeological park where visitors can explore Alexandria's ancient Great Harbor from glass-bottomed boats.

Main Idea	1		
		Answer	**Score**
	Mark the *main idea*	M	15
	Mark the statement that is *too broad*	B	5
	Mark the statement that is *too narrow*	N	5

a. Underwater archaeology has helped to reveal Alexandria's Great Harbor. ☐ _____

b. An ancient underwater city exists in Alexandria, Egypt. ☐ _____

c. Satellites help archaeologists map Alexandria's Great Harbor. ☐ _____

114

Subject Matter　　2　This passage primarily focuses on
- ☐ a. a history of Alexandria.
- ☐ b. the excavation of Alexandria.
- ☐ c. the excavation of Alexandria's harbor.
- ☐ d. creating archaeological parks.　　　　　_____

Supporting Details　　3　The Great Harbor was destroyed by
- ☐ a. tourists.
- ☐ b. archaeologists.
- ☐ c. earthquakes and tidal waves.
- ☐ d. shallow water.　　　　　_____

Conclusion　　4　The underwater excavation of the Great Harbor has been
- ☐ a. effortless.
- ☐ b. complicated.
- ☐ c. useless.
- ☐ d. simple.　　　　　_____

Clarifying Devices　　5　The second paragraph of this passage
- ☐ a. narrates a story.
- ☐ b. explains a process.
- ☐ c. describes a site.
- ☐ d. argues in favor of archaeology.　　　　　_____

Vocabulary in Context　　6　In this passage, <u>generate</u> means to
- ☐ a. create electric power.
- ☐ b. describe.
- ☐ c. bring into existence.
- ☐ d. remove from the ground.　　　　　_____

Add your scores for questions 1–6. Enter the total here and on the graph on page 160.　　**Total Score**　　_____

58 Please Continue

In 1963 Stanley Milgram, a psychologist at Yale University, conducted a study focusing on the conflict between obedience to authority and personal conscience. This was nearly two decades after the World War II Nuremberg war criminal trials in which the defense of those accused of genocide was based on "obedience." The accused said they were just following the orders of their superiors.

In Milgram's experiment, so-called "teachers," who were the unknowing subjects of the experiment, were to administer an increasingly stronger electric shock to "learners." The <u>fictitious</u> story given to these "teachers" was that the experiment was exploring the effects of punishment on learning behavior. Unknown to the "teacher," the "learner" was really an actor pretending to be uncomfortable as the shocks increased. The teacher was to read a list of two word pairs and ask the learner to say them back. If the learner answered correctly, they moved on to the next word pair. If the answer was incorrect, the teacher was to shock the learner. Shocks began at 15 volts and went up to 450 volts.

At times, worried teachers questioned the experimenter, asking who was taking responsibility for harming the learner. The experimenter replied that he assumed full responsibility. At this, the teachers seemed able to continue. When teachers asked if they should continue increasing the shocks, the experimenter verbally encouraged them.

To Milgram's surprise and the surprise of his colleagues, 65 percent of the teachers obeyed orders to punish the learner to the very end of the 450-volt scale, and no teachers stopped before reaching 300 volts. One of Milgram's conclusions was that ordinary people, simply doing their jobs, can become agents in a destructive process.

Main Idea	1		
		Answer	**Score**
Mark the *main idea*		M	15
Mark the statement that is *too broad*		B	5
Mark the statement that is *too narrow*		N	5

   a. Milgram's experiment tested obedience to authority. □ _____

   b. Experimenters said they took full responsibility for harm to learners. □ _____

   c. Psychological experiments can prove or disprove theories. □ _____

Subject Matter   **2**   This passage mainly focuses on
    ☐ a. the life of Stanley Milgram.
    ☐ b. a definition of social psychology.
    ☐ c. a summary of a psychological experiment.
    ☐ d. a history of the Nuremberg trials.   _____

Supporting   **3**   The "learner" in Milgram's experimenter was really
Details
    ☐ a. a war criminal.
    ☐ b. Stanley Milgram.
    ☐ c. an experimenter.
    ☐ d. an actor.   _____

Conclusion   **4**   Most of the "teachers" in the experiment decided
    ☐ a. it was all right to inflict pain if someone else
        told them it was.
    ☐ b. 450 volts of electricity was a large jolt.
    ☐ c. that they liked to cause pain.
    ☐ d. that they resented being told what to do.   _____

Clarifying   **5**   The quotation marks around the words *learner*
Devices   and *teacher* in this passage mean that
    ☐ a. the real meaning of these words is not what is
        meant here.
    ☐ b. this is quoted material.
    ☐ c. these are titles.
    ☐ d. these are special technical words.   _____

Vocabulary   **6**   In this passage, <u>fictitious</u> means
in Context
    ☐ a. not true; made up.
    ☐ b. elaborate and complicated.
    ☐ c. assumed in order to deceive.
    ☐ d. experimental.   _____

Add your scores for questions 1–6. Enter the total here   **Total**
and on the graph on page 160.   **Score**   _____

59 The Mystery of the Ancient Ones

The mystery of the prehistoric Native American people known as the Anasazi begins with their very name, because no evidence exists telling what these people called themselves. *Anasazi* is a Navajo word meaning "ancient ones," but most Navajo <u>aver</u> that the word means "ancient enemies" while some translate the word to mean "ancient ancestors." The Hopi word for these early people is *Hisatsinom,* which means "those-who-came-before." And they did come before, having lived in the Southwest United States from before A.D. 1 to A.D. 1275.

The deep canyons, rock palisades, high mesas, and open desert of the Four Corners area, where Colorado, Utah, Arizona, and New Mexico converge, were home to this remarkable group of people. The dramatic remains of tens of thousands of Anasazi rock and mud dwellings document their building techniques. They constructed masonry homes that varied from simple underground pit structures to large multistoried villages. We know that the population grew and clustered in small villages. We suspect that climatic changes and conflict with neighboring groups caused occasional shifts in settlement.

The Anasazi were highly skilled potters. Beautifully decorated bowls, ladles, and mugs have been discovered in Anasazi ruins. The Anasazi also produced fine baskets, ornaments, woven goods, and tools and had a trade network extending to central Mexico. We also know that they hunted game, gathered wild plants, and grew corn, beans, and squash.

But archaeologists still puzzle over the unsolved riddles of the Anasazi. Why, by A.D. 1300, had they abandoned the Four Corners area, and (an even greater question) where did they go? Only time and further archaeological research can solve this mystery of the ancient ones.

Main Idea 1		Answer	Score
Mark the *main idea*		M	15
Mark the statement that is *too broad*		B	5
Mark the statement that is *too narrow*		N	5

a. It is not known why the rich culture of the Anasazi died out. ☐ ____

b. The Anasazi were a prehistoric culture. ☐ ____

c. The Anasazi built and traded. ☐ ____

Subject Matter   2   This passage focuses mostly on
- ☐ a. the Four Corners area.
- ☐ b. what we know and don't know about the Anasazi.
- ☐ c. Anasazi buildings.
- ☐ d. what the word *Anasazi* means.

_____

Supporting Details   3   The Anasazi disappeared before
- ☐ a. A.D. 1.
- ☐ b. A.D. 1300.
- ☐ c. A.D. 1750.
- ☐ d. A.D. 1900.

_____

Conclusion   4   The things the Anasazi most likely traded were
- ☐ a. sheep.
- ☐ b. building materials.
- ☐ c. beads and skins.
- ☐ d. pottery, baskets, and woven goods.

_____

Clarifying Devices   5   The term *Four Corners* is explained by
- ☐ a. describing its mountains.
- ☐ b. telling where it is.
- ☐ c. narrating a story about it.
- ☐ d. summarizing its history.

_____

Vocabulary in Context   6   <u>Aver</u> means to
- ☐ a. assert to be true.
- ☐ b. avoid.
- ☐ c. provide a written history of.
- ☐ d. construct.

_____

Add your scores for questions 1–6. Enter the total here and on the graph on page 160.   **Total Score** _____

60 Bigger and Bigger

Throughout the 20th century, Japanese towns and cities grew rapidly. Today about 80 percent of the Japanese people live in urban areas. The growth of towns and cities, called *urbanization,* happens in two ways. One way is by natural population increase, when more people are born than die. The second way is by rural-urban migration, when people move to the cities from the country. As cities prosper and grow, industries and services that involve many people both as workers and consumers grow to meet the needs of the increasing population. New industries and services emerge to support the growing businesses, and the region experiences an upward spiral of growth.

The urban areas on the Japanese island of Honshu continue to grow as they attract more people, industry, and business. These urban areas contain nearly two-thirds of Japan's population and manufacturing. City suburbs are filling in the rural spaces between the towns and cities, and Japan's efficient and fast transportation system links them all.

Four major cities on Honshu—Tokyo, Kawasaki, Chiba, and Yokohama—have grown together into one of Japan's largest urban areas. Two other large urban areas have developed on Honshu. The area around the city of Nagoya forms one, and the cities of Osaka, Kyoto, and Kobe form the other. At the present time, these three areas are growing toward one another to form one long, enormous urban area. A single urban system this large is called a megalopolis. This Japanese megalopolis on Honshu, stretching from Tokyo in the east all the way to Kobe in the west, is called the Tokaido megalopolis.

Main Idea	1		Answer	Score
	Mark the *main idea*		M	15
	Mark the statement that is *too broad*		B	5
	Mark the statement that is *too narrow*		N	5

a. Japanese urbanization is leading to a megalopolis. ☐ _____

b. Japan has experienced rural-urban migration. ☐ _____

c. Japan has large urban areas. ☐ _____

Subject Matter   **2**   This passage is mostly about
- ☐ a. what a megalopolis is.
- ☐ b. a system of rural-urban migration.
- ☐ c. how a megalopolis is forming in Japan.
- ☐ d. a fast transportation system in Japan.   _____

Supporting Details   **3**   The urban areas of Honshu
- ☐ a. are shrinking.
- ☐ b. contain two-thirds of Japan's population.
- ☐ c. are not part of Japan.
- ☐ d. are far from the megalopolis.   _____

Conclusion   **4**   A megalopolis is the result of
- ☐ a. natural growth.
- ☐ b. deliberate planning.
- ☐ c. fast commuter trains.
- ☐ d. poverty.   _____

Clarifying Devices   **5**   The phrase *an upward spiral* in the last sentence of the first paragraph is a metaphor for
- ☐ a. decreasing population and industry.
- ☐ b. circular population.
- ☐ c. repetitious numbers of workers and consumers.
- ☐ d. ever-increasing population and industry.   _____

Vocabulary in Context   **6**   In this passage, <u>emerge</u> means to
- ☐ a. become connected.
- ☐ b. come into being.
- ☐ c. become well known.
- ☐ d. meet the needs of people.   _____

Add your scores for questions 1–6. Enter the total here and on the graph on page 160.   **Total Score**   _____

61 Very Separate, Very Unequal

Apartheid was the South African policy of racial segregation that benefited the white minority and discriminated against the black majority. From 1948 to 1994, apartheid helped the white minority in South Africa keep political power.

What were some of the effects of apartheid? Apartheid forcibly removed millions of black people into predominately black homelands and townships that were far from the nearest town or city. Schools, health care, water, sanitation, and transportation in these areas were <u>rudimentary</u> at best. Most of the people in the settlements were impoverished and had little opportunity for employment. Young men migrated to the white areas to work in the mines and factories, while the elderly, children, women, and disabled people remained in the homelands.

How did the apartheid system begin to crumble? A number of foreign governments and human rights organizations demanded an end to the system. Trade sanctions and divestment (the withdrawal of investment by foreign companies) pressured the government to change its policies. However, the biggest challenge came from within South Africa. The African National Congress, the KwaZulu-dominated Inkatha group, the churches of South Africa, and the trade union movements all spoke out for a democratic future.

When did apartheid finally come to an end? The politics of apartheid ended in 1994 when South Africa held its first democratic election. All South Africans were able to vote for the first time. The result was the election of the African National Congress candidate, Nelson Mandela, as South Africa's first black president.

Main Idea	1	Answer	Score
	Mark the *main idea*	M	15
	Mark the statement that is *too broad*	B	5
	Mark the statement that is *too narrow*	N	5

a. Under apartheid, black people were moved to townships. ☐ _____

b. South Africa has a troubled history. ☐ _____

c. South Africa was forced to dismantle its policy of apartheid ☐ _____

Score 15 points for each correct answer.　　　　　　　　**Score**

Subject Matter　　2　This passage is mostly about how apartheid
- [ ] a. promised a democratic future.
- [ ] b. discriminated against black people.
- [ ] c. created jobs in mines and factories.
- [ ] d. pressured governments into trade
agreements.　　　　　　　　　　　_____

Supporting Details　　3　People living in the settlements
- [ ] a. worked in mines and factories.
- [ ] b. were poor and had little work.
- [ ] c. were only women.
- [ ] d. were members of the African National
Congress.　　　　　　　　　　　_____

Conclusion　　4　Apartheid ended because of
- [ ] a. the white minority's desire for a black
president.
- [ ] b. full employment opportunities for blacks.
- [ ] c. the growing prosperity within South Africa.
- [ ] d. economic and political pressures.　　_____

Clarifying Devices　　5　The questions at the beginnings of paragraphs
- [ ] a. are not intended to be answered.
- [ ] b. introduce the topics of the paragraphs.
- [ ] c. come from South African newspapers.
- [ ] d. are not related to what follows them.　_____

Vocabulary in Context　　6　In this passage, <u>rudimentary</u> means
- [ ] a. undeveloped.
- [ ] b. discourteous.
- [ ] c. completely adequate.
- [ ] d. to be learned or studied first.　　_____

Add your scores for questions 1–6. Enter the total here　　**Total**
and on the graph on page 160.　　**Score**　　_____

62 You Have the Right to Remain Silent

Ernesto Miranda, sent to jail for the kidnapping and assault of a woman in Phoenix, Arizona, appealed his case to a higher court on the grounds that he had been forced to incriminate himself. The facts before the U.S. Supreme Court were that Miranda was <u>interrogated</u> at length following his arrest and that he signed a confession that was used to convict him. Miranda's lawyer argued that the confession had been forced and that the police had not warned Miranda that he did not have to answer. Miranda was also not told that anything he said voluntarily could be used against him in court. This, Miranda's lawyer insisted, was unconstitutional.

On June 16, 1966, the Supreme Court agreed, ordered a retrial for Miranda, and issued the following majority opinion.

> Prior to any questioning, the person must be warned that he has the right to remain silent, that any statement he does make may be used as evidence against him, and that he has a right to the presence of an attorney, either retained or appointed. The defendant may waive effectuation of these rights, provided the waiver is made voluntarily, knowingly, and intelligently. If, however, he indicates in any manner and at any stage of the process that he wishes to consult with an attorney before speaking, there can be no questioning.

This decision led to the Miranda Rule. Police must inform a suspect of his or her rights, which are the right to remain silent and the right to have an attorney present.

Ernesto Miranda was retried, convicted again, and served prison time until he was paroled in 1972. In 1976 Miranda, who was 34 years old, was stabbed to death during a fight in a bar.

Main Idea	1		
		Answer	**Score**
	Mark the *main idea*	M	15
	Mark the statement that is *too broad*	B	5
	Mark the statement that is *too narrow*	N	5

a. The U.S. Supreme Court heard Ernesto Miranda's appeal. ☐ _____

b. Ernesto Miranda was sent to jail for kidnapping and assault. ☐ _____

c. The Supreme Court's Miranda decision clarified the rights of a crime suspect. ☐ _____

Score 15 points for each correct answer.   **Score**

Subject Matter   2   The Miranda case had mostly to do with the
- [ ] a. rights of police officers.
- [ ] b. rights of an accused attorney.
- [ ] c. rights of an arrested individual.
- [ ] d. guilt or innocence of Ernesto Miranda.   _____

Supporting Details   3   Ernesto Miranda appealed his case on the grounds that
- [ ] a. he was not guilty.
- [ ] b. he had been forced to incriminate himself.
- [ ] c. police had not informed him that he was under arrest.
- [ ] d. he had not signed a confession.   _____

Conclusion   4   The U.S. Supreme Court agreed that Miranda's rights had been violated and that this was
- [ ] a. questionable.
- [ ] b. interrogation procedure.
- [ ] c. unconstitutional.
- [ ] d. newsworthy.   _____

Clarifying Devices   5   The indenting of the third paragraph on both right and left margins tells the reader that this is
- [ ] a. quoted material.
- [ ] b. legal jargon.
- [ ] c. paraphrased material.
- [ ] d. a list.   _____

Vocabulary in Context   6   The word <u>interrogated</u> means
- [ ] a. warned.
- [ ] b. interrupted.
- [ ] c. opposed.
- [ ] d. questioned.   _____

Add your scores for questions 1–6. Enter the total here and on the graph on page 160.   **Total Score**   _____

63 1968: A Watershed Year

Some historians mark 1968 as a watershed year in the U.S. Civil Rights movement. They see it as a turning point in the flow of events and a changing point in the way people thought about their country's problems. One changing point of view was that Civil Rights demonstrations had gotten out of hand. Many people in the United States called for law and order, but violence seemed to be escalating. Malcolm X, a leader of the Nation of Islam who proclaimed that blacks needed to be strong and independent and that they should use all available means to achieve equality and justice, had been assassinated in 1965. And in 1968 Rev. Martin Luther King Jr., a founder of the Southern Christian Leadership Conference and the last best hope for change through nonviolent means, was also shot down.

People in the United States had become accustomed to nonviolent protesters. Now they were confronted by more-militant activists such as Stokely Carmichael and by the Black Power movement. The clear and single-purpose fight against segregation <u>waned</u> as issues such as poverty and discrimination came to the forefront. In 1966 and 1967 poverty, rage, and hopelessness prompted riots in more than 100 U.S. cities, destroying the neighborhoods that Civil Rights activists were trying to improve. The King assassination brought more rage and rioting across the country.

The United States was also sending troops to Vietnam during this period, and military personnel were dying. The Tet offensive in January 1968 sparked the growing antiwar effort against U.S. military involvement in Vietnam. This new cause siphoned increasing attention, energy, and resources away from the Civil Rights movement.

From 1968 on, Civil Rights concerns about equality would broaden to include basic human rights, such as decent homes, health care, jobs, and education.

Main Idea	1	Answer	Score
	Mark the *main idea*	M	15
	Mark the statement that is *too broad*	B	5
	Mark the statement that is *too narrow*	N	5

a. People's views of the Civil Rights movement changed around 1968. ☐ _____

b. The Civil Rights movement went through some changes. ☐ _____

c. In 1968 many Americans were dying in Vietnam. ☐ _____

Subject Matter   2   This passage is mostly about
☐ a. Malcolm X and Martin Luther King Jr.
☐ b. causes of change in the Civil Rights movement.
☐ c. protests against the Vietnam War.
☐ d. violent protests and counterprotests.   _____

Supporting Details   3   The Vietnam War affected the Civil Rights movement by
☐ a. destroying black neighborhoods.
☐ b. taking attention away from it.
☐ c. resolving many Civil Rights issues.
☐ d. requiring that Civil Rights leaders be drafted.   _____

Conclusion   4   The last paragraph suggests that
☐ a. Civil Rights no longer concern Americans.
☐ b. the scope of the civil rights movement changed.
☐ c. the Civil Rights movement is over.
☐ d. the Civil Rights movement in the United States was ineffective.   _____

Clarifying Devices   5   Stokely Carmichael is given as an example of
☐ a. a militant activist.
☐ b. a nonviolent protester.
☐ c. an assassinated Civil Rights leader.
☐ d. an antiwar protester.   _____

Vocabulary in Context   6   <u>Waned</u> means
☐ a. became ill.
☐ b. increased the cost of.
☐ c. lost importance.
☐ d. disagreed.   _____

Add your scores for questions 1–6. Enter the total here and on the graph on page 160.   **Total Score**   _____

64 Good, Bad, or In-between

Sigmund Freud's work as a psychological theorist generated many terms and concepts. Among the most essential terms are those describing what he conceived to be the three major components of personality: the id, the ego, and the superego. For Freud, the human mind functioned as a battleground. It was the scene of a never-ending struggle between the three opposing forces of id, ego, and superego as they struggled for supremacy of the human personality.

The id is what Freud called in his earlier writing "the unconscious." It represents blind impulse and energy, and it operates according to the pleasure principle. The id demands immediate satisfaction regardless of circumstances and possible undesirable effects.

The ego represents reason and common sense. The ego understands that immediate gratification is usually impossible and often unwise. It operates according to the reality principle. With the formation of the ego, the individual becomes a self, instead of merely an animal that is driven only by urges and needs. The ego may temporarily repress the urges of the id with the fear of external punishment. Eventually, however, a person internalizes the punishment—it becomes part of him or her.

The superego is this internalization of punishment. The superego uses guilt and self-reproach to enforce rules and produce good behavior. When a person does something acceptable to the superego, the person experiences pride and self-satisfaction. The superego represents the rules and standards of adult society. It is often described as the conscience, but it is much more <u>punitive</u>, unforgiving, and irrational than a conscience.

Main Idea	1		
		Answer	**Score**
Mark the *main idea*		M	15
Mark the statement that is *too broad*		B	5
Mark the statement that is *too narrow*		N	5

a. Sigmund Freud was a psychological theorist. ☐ _____

b. Individuals are driven in part by urges and needs. ☐ _____

c. Freud's theory of personality has three major components. ☐ _____

Subject Matter   2   This passage focuses on
- [ ] a. the only theory of human personality.
- [ ] b. Freud's theory of human personality.
- [ ] c. the ego and the superego.
- [ ] d. the history of human personality study.   _____

Supporting Details   3   The ego operates according to
- [ ] a. the reality principle.
- [ ] b. the pleasure principle.
- [ ] c. an economic principle.
- [ ] d. a self-satisfaction principle.   _____

Conclusion   4   According to Freud's theories, which part of the personality would most likely be responsible for developing the rules and regulations for a school?
- [ ] a. id
- [ ] b. ego
- [ ] c. superego
- [ ] d. unconscious   _____

Clarifying Devices   5   Which of the following is a simile for Freud's view of the human mind?
- [ ] a. It is like a battleground.
- [ ] b. It is like an animal.
- [ ] c. It is like a blind impulse.
- [ ] d. It is like a person experiencing self-satisfaction.   _____

Vocabulary in Context   6   The word <u>punitive</u> means
- [ ] a. forgetful.
- [ ] b. sensitive.
- [ ] c. thoughtful.
- [ ] d. seeking to punish.   _____

Add your scores for questions 1–6. Enter the total here and on the graph on page 160.   **Total Score**   _____

65 Looking for Mr. Spenser

Kilcolman Castle, on Kilcolman Hill in County Cork, Ireland, is one of hundreds of small castles found throughout the Irish countryside. But Kilcolman Castle had a famous resident in the late 1500s. He was the English poet Edmund Spenser. Kilcolman Castle is where Spenser wrote *The Faerie Queene,* considered to be the greatest epic poem of the Elizabethan Age. Four hundred years later, in the late 1990s, Irish graduate students, volunteers, architects, archaeologists, and historians searched for clues of Spenser's presence in the now-ruined castle.

The first task was to look at the surviving masonry and the surrounding terrain. Shrubbery and ivy were cleared away, cattle manure was removed from the cellar, and the land was surveyed. Over the next three years, a geophysical survey was undertaken to locate buried archaeological features. A geophysical survey is done by measuring variations in the soil's resistance to electricity every three feet. The purpose is to locate buried walls and pits. A laptop computer helps the archaeologist map the finds right in the field.

Although the site proved to be rich in <u>domestic</u> artifacts, such as fragments of pottery from storage and serving vessels and a pewter spoon handle and dish fragment, few artifacts could be associated with Spenser. Among personal items found that may have belonged to the poet were pins, a spur, the bronze tip of a dagger scabbard, and metal fittings for furniture or trunks. The four seasons of field work did, however, produce a plan of the castle enclosure, reveal the different construction phases of the tower-house, locate and identify other structures, and keep alive the possibility of learning still more about life in the Elizabethan age.

Main Idea 1		Answer	Score
Mark the *main idea*		M	15
Mark the statement that is *too broad*		B	5
Mark the statement that is *too narrow*		N	5

a. Archaeologists are aided in their work by computers.	☐	_____
b. Archaeologists have studied castles in Ireland	☐	_____
c. A ruined castle in Ireland helped to reveal Elizabethan life.	☐	_____

Subject Matter   **2**   This passage is mainly about
- [ ] a. Spenser and his poetry.
- [ ] b. castle construction.
- [ ] c. the Elizabethan age.
- [ ] d. an archaeological project.   _____

Supporting   **3**   One of the uncovered artifacts that may have
Details   belonged to Edmund Spenser was
- [ ] a. a map.
- [ ] b. a pewter spoon handle.
- [ ] c. the bronze tip of a dagger scabbard.
- [ ] d. a laptop computer.   _____

Conclusion   **4**   The excavation at Kilcolman Castle
- [ ] a. uncovered no valuable information.
- [ ] b. uncovered information but not what the
        archaeologists were looking for.
- [ ] c. completely changed people's views about life
        in Ireland.
- [ ] d. was a waste of time and resources.   _____

Clarifying   **5**   The word *although* at the beginning of the third
Devices   paragraph signals
- [ ] a. an example.
- [ ] b. a contrast.
- [ ] c. an argument.
- [ ] d. a reason.   _____

Vocabulary   **6**   In this passage, <u>domestic</u> means
in Context
- [ ] a. related to the home.
- [ ] b. a household servant.
- [ ] c. tame.
- [ ] d. not of a foreign country.   _____

Add your scores for questions 1–6. Enter the total here   **Total**
and on the graph on page 160.   **Score**   _____

66 Suu Kyi's Struggle

The prestigious 1991 Nobel Peace Prize went to Daw Aung San Suu Kyi (dah ông san sōo chē). The Nobel Committee chose to honor her for her "nonviolent struggle for democracy and human rights." Suu Kyi could not be present in Oslo, Norway, on December 10, 1991, to accept her award because she was under house arrest in the capital city of Yangon, Myanmar (the former Rangoon, Burma), in Southeast Asia.

Suu Kyi's political activities as leader of the National League of Democracy (NLD) began in 1988 when, at the age of 46, she returned to Burma to assist her ill mother. Her father, U Aung San, had fought for the liberation of Burma, first from the British and then from the Japanese in World War II. He was assassinated in 1947, when Suu Kyi was two years old.

When Suu Kyi returned to Burma, she was propelled into politics by the violent protests in that country. The protests forced the resignation of U Ne Win, the country's longtime military strongman. Suu Kyi's political involvement resulted in her being placed under house arrest in 1989 and kept isolated for six years. The governing military council held parliamentary elections in May 1990, and in spite of Suu Kyi's isolation, her party, the NLD, won 392 of the 485 contested seats. The military council ignored the results.

In announcing her selection for the Nobel Peace Prize, the committee said, "Suu Kyi's struggle is one of the most extraordinary examples of civil courage in Asia in recent decades." Although no longer under house arrest, her activities are still closely monitored and her closest supporters are in jail, but Daw Aung San Suu Kyi remains committed to the struggle for a free and democratic Burma.

Main Idea	1	Answer	Score
	Mark the *main idea*	M	15
	Mark the statement that is *too broad*	B	5
	Mark the statement that is *too narrow*	N	5

a. The Nobel Peace Prize was awarded to Suu Kyi for her efforts to bring democracy to Burma. ☐ _____

b. Many have struggled for freedom in Burma. ☐ _____

c. Suu Kyi is the leader of the NLD. ☐

Score 15 points for each correct answer.   Score

Subject Matter   2   This passage is mostly about
- ☐ a. how Suu Kyi caused political upheaval.
- ☐ b. Suu Kyi's family.
- ☐ c. why Suu Kyi won the Nobel Prize.
- ☐ d. the meaning of human rights.   _____

Supporting Details   3   Suu Kyi is the daughter of
- ☐ a. U Ne Win, Burmese military strongman.
- ☐ b. Yangon Myanmar, the former Rangoon.
- ☐ c. U Aung San, who was active in the liberation of Burma.
- ☐ d. a Nobel Peace Prize winner.   _____

Conclusion   4   The writer of this passage considers Suu Kyi to be a
- ☐ a. violent protester.
- ☐ b. strong, committed leader.
- ☐ c. political troublemaker.
- ☐ d. person with limited influence.   _____

Clarifying Devices   5   The first and final paragraphs of this passage are organizationally related because they both
- ☐ a. tell of Suu Kyi's family.
- ☐ b. describe Suu Kyi's house arrest.
- ☐ c. use Suu Kyi's full name.
- ☐ d. explain what the Nobel Prize was awarded for.   _____

Vocabulary in Context   6   The word <u>liberation</u> means
- ☐ a. freedom.
- ☐ b. honor.
- ☐ c. recognition.
- ☐ d. reorganization.   _____

Add your scores for questions 1–6. Enter the total here and on the graph on page 160.

Total Score   _____

133

67 Domestic Violence

The National Coalition Against Domestic Violence defines domestic violence as "a pattern of behavior with the effect of establishing power and control over another person through fear and <u>intimidation</u>." Domestic violence is viewed as any violent or threatening behavior between family members. This includes abuse between former husbands and wives and between unmarried partners who live together. It is the leading cause of injury to women in the United States, with more than an estimated 2 million women being severely beaten in their homes each year. According to the U.S. Justice Department, 94 percent of violence between partners involves a man beating a woman.

Violence in the home was not publicly addressed until the 1970s, when women began to demand their rights. Women working together established local shelters and domestic abuse hotlines. They pressured states to enact and enforce domestic abuse prevention laws. Groups of battered women filed class-action suits against police departments and court officers who failed to arrest and prosecute abusers. Domestic violence began to be viewed as a crime, and cases were moved from the civil to the criminal courts.

Long-overdue education and training programs about the nature and effects of domestic abuse became available for police officers, prosecutors, and judges. Programs were also aimed at the abusive men to help them understand and stop being abusers. And domestic violence awareness programs were started in schools. With domestic violence out in the open, there is increased awareness, better prevention, and more help for those who are abused.

Main Idea   1

	Answer	Score
Mark the *main idea*	M	15
Mark the statement that is *too broad*	B	5
Mark the statement that is *too narrow*	N	5

a. Violence and threatening behavior are never appropriate. ☐ _____

b. Domestic violence has been recognized as a crime, and steps have been taken to deal with it. ☐ _____

c. Programs for abusive men are aimed at helping them change their behavior. ☐ _____

Score 15 points for each correct answer. Score

Subject Matter 2 This passage is mostly about
☐ a. shelters for battered women.
☐ b. programs for abusive men.
☐ c. court cases about domestic violence.
☐ d. domestic violence and efforts to stop it. _____

Supporting Details 3 According to this passage, domestic violence
☐ a. is the result of alcoholism.
☐ b. affects about 20 million U.S. women.
☐ c. started in the 1970s.
☐ d. is the leading cause of injury to women. _____

Conclusion 4 The last sentence of this passage suggests that the problem
☐ a. can be reduced.
☐ b. is too difficult to solve.
☐ c. no longer exists.
☐ d. is not big enough to worry about. _____

Clarifying Devices 5 The information in this passage is organized through
☐ a. personal narrative.
☐ b. problem and solution.
☐ c. fact and opinion.
☐ d. case study. _____

Vocabulary in Context 6 In this passage, <u>intimidation</u> means
☐ a. closeness.
☐ b. threats of violence.
☐ c. lack of tolerance.
☐ d. disagreement. _____

Add your scores for questions 1–6. Enter the total here and on the graph on page 160. Total Score _____

68 Unwritten History

The integration of history and archaeology has led to the study of people who have often been denied a voice in traditional history because of race, class, or gender. The historical archaeologist challenges traditional <u>interpretations</u> of the past and questions written sources of history. The historical archaeologist goes directly to the people for evidence of the people's history. The following two examples show historical archaeology at work.

While digging a site for an office tower in lower Manhattan, New York City, workers unearthed the bones of some 400 bodies buried in an 18th-century cemetery for African slaves. The information held in this cemetery provided data about the health of enslaved Africans prior to the American Revolution. Half of the 400 skeletons belonged to children under the age of 12. Nearly half of those were infants. Of the children who survived infancy, half showed signs of illness and malnutrition. Evidence of cultural continuity from Africa to the New World was found in a heart-shaped design of tacks hammered into one coffin lid. The design is thought to be a ritual symbol of the Akan people of Ghana and Ivory Coast.

The second example is found in the excavations at Southern plantations by Charles H. Fairbanks in the 1960s. Fairbanks's research pieced together information from the enslaved people. By excavating slave cabins, he found that Africans ate a variety of wild local plants, hunted game with guns, trapped and ate raccoons and opossums, caught mullet and catfish in tidal streams, and cooked in their homes. And like the evidence of the New York coffin design, Fairbanks's evidence also showed that African culture and identity—expressed in the people's pottery, food, and architecture—had been preserved in the New World.

Main Idea	1		
		Answer	**Score**
	Mark the *main idea*	M	15
	Mark the statement that is *too broad*	B	5
	Mark the statement that is *too narrow*	N	5

a. Historical archaeologists study cemeteries and plantations. ☐ _____

b. Historical archaeologists study the nonwritten evidence of people lives. ☐ _____

c. Historical archaeology is a field of study. ☐ _____

Score 15 points for each correct answer.   **Score**

Subject Matter   **2**   This passage mostly focuses on
- ☐ a. why historical archaeology is important.
- ☐ b. what historical archaeology can show about poor or enslaved people.
- ☐ c. how historical archaeology is changing today.
- ☐ d. comparing classical archaeology and historical archaeology.

_____

Supporting Details   **3**   The Manhattan cemetery yielded information about the
- ☐ a. health of African slaves.
- ☐ b. diet of African slaves.
- ☐ c. clothing of African slaves.
- ☐ d. literacy rate of African slaves.

_____

Conclusion   **4**   Fairbanks's excavations show that slaves on Southern plantations
- ☐ a. often went hungry.
- ☐ b. were excellent cooks.
- ☐ c. had a fair amount of leisure time.
- ☐ d. had a varied diet.

_____

Clarifying Devices   **5**   The term _historical archaeology_ is explained through
- ☐ a. a dictionary definition.
- ☐ b. a question-and-answer format.
- ☐ c. definition and examples.
- ☐ d. comparison and contrast.

_____

Vocabulary in Context   **6**   In this passage, <u>interpretations</u> means
- ☐ a. questions.
- ☐ b. evaluations.
- ☐ c. translations.
- ☐ d. summaries.

_____

Add your scores for questions 1–6. Enter the total here and on the graph on page 160.   **Total Score** _____

69 Growing Your Brain

Jean Piaget (1896–1980), an influential experimenter and theorist in developmental psychology, identified changes in the way children think at different stages in their development. Piaget stated that there are four distinct periods of mental development and that each period involves increasingly more-complex thought processes.

The first stage is *sensorimotor.* It lasts from birth to the beginning of language, or about the first eighteen months of life. In this period of development, children function at a practical, nonsymbolic level.

The second stage is *preoperational.* It lasts from early childhood years up to the age of six or seven. This is a stage of egocentrism in which children are incapable of taking into account the point of view of others. They learn to use language, symbols, and mental imagery. Putting objects in sequence, from first to last or smallest to largest, is difficult, as is understanding past, present, and future.

The *concrete operational* stage lasts from the elementary school years until the age of 11. Children in this stage normally acquire the ability to organize and relate experiences into an ordered pattern. They begin to understand reversibility—the idea that they can think backwards from the end to the beginning of a process. They also understand multiple classification, which allows them to classify items according to more than one <u>attribute</u>.

The *formal operational* stage begins at about the age of 11 and lasts through the middle school years. A new form of thinking emerges as children begin to manipulate symbols and ideas and to think abstractly. They can develop and test hypotheses, make inferences, draw conclusions, and engage in problem solving.

Main Idea	1	Answer	Score
Mark the *main idea*		M	15
Mark the statement that is *too broad*		B	5
Mark the statement that is *too narrow*		N	5

a. New thinking emerges for children in the middle school years. ☐ _____

b. Theories about mental processes are part of the study of psychology. ☐ _____

c. Piaget's theory identified four stages of intellectual development. ☐ _____

Subject Matter　**2**　The information in this passage has mostly to do with the field of
- [ ] a. philosophy.
- [ ] b. interpersonal relations.
- [ ] c. sociology.
- [ ] d. child psychology.

　　　　　　　　　　　　　　　　　　　　　　　　_____

Supporting Details　**3**　Between the ages of 7 and 11, children are likely to be in the
- [ ] a. sensorimotor stage.
- [ ] b. preoperational stage.
- [ ] c. concrete operational stage.
- [ ] d. formal operational stage.

　　　　　　　　　　　　　　　　　　　　　　　　_____

Conclusion　**4**　Children in the preoperational stage would be most likely to
- [ ] a. refuse to share toys with others.
- [ ] b. enjoy a game that required helping a partner.
- [ ] c. group their toys into the categories of vehicles, dolls, and games.
- [ ] d. make an inference from a story they hear.

　　　　　　　　　　　　　　　　　　　　　　　　_____

Clarifying Devices　**5**　Words like *sensorimotor* and *formal operational* are italicized in this passage because they
- [ ] a. are words Piaget made up.
- [ ] b. are key words.
- [ ] c. represent the exact words of a speaker.
- [ ] d. are part of a list.

　　　　　　　　　　　　　　　　　　　　　　　　_____

Vocabulary in Context　**6**　In this passage, <u>attribute</u> means
- [ ] a. give credit to.
- [ ] b. share with a group.
- [ ] c. quality.
- [ ] d. belief.

　　　　　　　　　　　　　　　　　　　　　　　　_____

Add your scores for questions 1–6. Enter the total here and on the graph on page 160.　　**Total Score**　_____

70 Psychological Research

Psychologists use a research approach just as other scientists do. They develop hypotheses, which are possible explanations for what they have observed, and they use scientific methods to test the hypotheses. There are three main techniques used in psychological research.

Naturalistic observation, the first technique, involves watching the behavior of human beings and animals in their natural environment. The researcher looks for broad patterns of behavior. Psychologists conducting such studies try to observe a <u>representative</u> sample. This sample should be a large typical group that reflects the total population. Naturalistic observation is usually used to gain insights and ideas for later testing.

Systematic assessment, the second technique, includes case histories, surveys or public opinion polls, and standardized tests. These are used to examine people's thoughts, feelings, and personality traits. Systematic assessments enable psychologists to gather information that they could not get by naturalistic observation. The accuracy of this information depends on well-designed studies and truthful, complete responses from participating individuals.

The third technique, experimentation, allows scientists to test a theory under controlled conditions as they attempt to discover or confirm cause-and-effect relationships. The researcher randomly divides subjects into two groups. One group is the experimental group, and the other is the control group. The condition to be tested is changed only for the experimental group. If the experimental group behaves differently from the control group, then the tested condition probably caused the difference.

Main Idea	1		Answer	Score
	Mark the *main idea*		M	15
	Mark the statement that is *too broad*		B	5
	Mark the statement that is *too narrow*		N	5
	a. Psychologists research individual behavior.	☐		_____
	b. Psychologists develop and test hypotheses.	☐		_____
	c. Psychologists use three techniques in their scientific research.	☐		_____

Subject Matter   2   This passage is primarily focused on
    ☐ a. hypotheses, explanation, and observation.
    ☐ b. naturalistic observation, systematic assessment, and experimentation.
    ☐ c. people's thoughts, feelings, personalities.
    ☐ d. individual behavior and scientific manner.   _____

Supporting Details   3   Case histories, surveys, and standardized assessment are part of
    ☐ a. experimentation.
    ☐ b. naturalistic observation.
    ☐ c. systematic assessment.
    ☐ d. people's personality traits.   _____

Conclusion   4   A psychologist watching children at play on a school playground would most likely be using
    ☐ a. standardized testing.
    ☐ b. analysis of cause-and-effect relationships.
    ☐ c. experimentation.
    ☐ d. naturalistic observation.   _____

Clarifying Devices   5   The words *first, second,* and *third* in this passage alert the reader that
    ☐ a. this is the order of steps in a research study.
    ☐ b. this is the order of importance.
    ☐ c. these are items in a list of research techniques.
    ☐ d. these are the numbers of the paragraphs.   _____

Vocabulary in Context   6   The word <u>representative</u> in this passage means
    ☐ a. large.
    ☐ b. serve as an example of something.
    ☐ c. natural.
    ☐ d. a person appointed to speak for others.   _____

Add your scores for questions 1–6. Enter the total here and on the graph on page 160.   **Total Score**   _____

71 The End of a Friendship

Psychoanalytic theories are concerned with the dynamics of behavior. Each theory offers an explanation as to why people feel, think, and act as they do. Sigmund Freud (1856–1939) developed the method of therapy called psychoanalysis, and his theory influenced the work of other major personality theorists who worked or trained at the Vienna Psychoanalytic Society. One of these theorists was Carl Gustav Jung (1875–1961), who had met Freud in 1907. Early in his career, Jung used Freud's psychoanalytical theories and participated in the psychoanalytic movement. Jung, like Freud, stressed the effects of unconscious ideas on human behavior. However, a series of disagreements led Jung to break with Freud, and their friendship ended in 1913.

Jung believed Freud placed too much importance on sexual instincts. He could not agree with Freud that human energy is essentially sexual in nature, preferring to believe that sexuality is only one example of human psychic energy. Another disagreement Jung had with Freud was that Jung's analytic psychology was more spiritual and mystical than Freud's. Jung believed that personal growth occurred through spiritual rediscovery and renewal. In yet another area of disagreement Jung, unlike Freud, did not believe that personality was fixed by the end of childhood. For Jung, the process of developing a unique self that would fulfill one's <u>potential</u> continued throughout life. He thought that the self, which represented a harmony or balance between opposing parts of the personality, was the most important structure. The self, Jung believed, could only emerge after the inner conflicts were resolved. The result of these disagreements was Jung's development of an analytic theory that addressed not only mental illness but also spirituality, goals, and growth in adulthood.

Main Idea	1		
		Answer	**Score**
	Mark the *main idea*	M	15
	Mark the statement that is *too broad*	B	5
	Mark the statement that is *too narrow*	N	5
	a. Personality theorists Freud and Jung did not always agree.	☐	____
	b. Jung's theory of psychology was more spiritual than Freud's.	☐	____
	c. Freud and Jung developed personality theories.	☐	____

Score 15 points for each correct answer.   **Score**

Subject Matter   2   Another good title for this passage is
- [ ] a. How Psychoanalysis Began.
- [ ] b. Freud and Jung: A Lifelong Partnership.
- [ ] c. Freud and Jung: A Difference in Approach.
- [ ] d. What Is a Personality?   _____

Supporting   3   Jung was
Details
- [ ] a. trained in Freud's theories.
- [ ] b. one of Freud's teachers.
- [ ] c. a dissenter who did not believe in psychology.
- [ ] d. convinced that personality was fixed by the end of childhood.   _____

Conclusion   4   Jung's theories
- [ ] a. were the same as Freud's.
- [ ] b. had no points of agreement with Freud's.
- [ ] c. kept Freud's theories and expanded on them.
- [ ] d. differed in fundamental ways from Freud's.   _____

Clarifying   5   The basic pattern used to develop this passage is
Devices
- [ ] a. a personal narrative.
- [ ] b. chronological order.
- [ ] c. comparison and contrast.
- [ ] d. question and answer.   _____

Vocabulary   6   In this passage, <u>potential</u> means
in Context
- [ ] a. strength.
- [ ] b. capabilities.
- [ ] c. electric force.
- [ ] d. a drink used as a medicine.   _____

Add your scores for questions 1–6. Enter the total here   **Total**
and on the graph on page 160.   **Score**   _____

72 The Work of the WPA

The Great Depression that followed the stock market crash of 1929 saw hundreds of thousands of U.S. citizens out of work. In this era of great fear and despair, citizens looked desperately to the federal government for assistance. Of all the programs devised by President Roosevelt when he took office in 1932, few were more criticized—or had more lasting impact—than the Work Projects Administration, better known as the WPA.

The intent of the WPA, which functioned from 1935 to 1943, was to devise and administer public works projects to help relieve unemployment. The majority of these projects involved historic or artistic endeavors. The WPA's Writers Project, for example, was responsible not only for such practical works as state guidebooks but also for the compilation of historically valuable oral histories. Over 2,900 of these records were collected in 24 states. They provide an irreplaceable firsthand account of people's diets, customs, celebrations, and political and religious beliefs at the time.

The artworks created through the Federal Arts Project are one of the WPA's most lasting achievements. Out-of-work painters, both famous and unknown, created murals that beautified schools, libraries, and government buildings. WPA photographers traveled across the country, recording the hardships of life on small rural farms. When the United States entered World War II, WPA artists were enlisted to produce posters supporting the war effort. Many WPA artworks, including hundreds of small drawings depicting scenes of everyday life, still exist today.

Main Idea	1	Answer	Score
	Mark the *main idea*	M	15
	Mark the statement that is *too broad*	B	5
	Mark the statement that is *too narrow*	N	5

a. Government intervention can often help in times of crisis. ☐ _____

b. WPA artists painted murals in schools and libraries. ☐ _____

c. The WPA produced many valuable and lasting works. ☐ _____

Score 15 points for each correct answer. **Score**

Subject Matter 2 The passage is mainly about
    ☐ a. projects undertaken by the WPA.
    ☐ b. the effect of the Great Depression on the United States.
    ☐ c. how oral histories help us understand U.S. citizens of that period.
    ☐ d. WPA artists and photographers. _____

Supporting Details 3 WPA photographers tried to
    ☐ a. create artistic works that could hang in museums.
    ☐ b. record the hard life on U.S. farms.
    ☐ c. show the beauty of the natural landscape.
    ☐ d. help the war effort. _____

Conclusion 4 This passage suggests that the WPA
    ☐ a. trained artists before it sent them out to work.
    ☐ b. had several smaller organizations working within it.
    ☐ c. was President Roosevelt's favorite project.
    ☐ d. will some day be reorganized and help people again. _____

Clarifying Devices 5 The author develops this passage mainly through
    ☐ a. a narrative about a WPA worker.
    ☐ b. comparison and contrast.
    ☐ c. a persuasive argument.
    ☐ d. examples. _____

Vocabulary in Context 6 The word <u>compilation</u> means
    ☐ a. distribution.
    ☐ b. separation.
    ☐ c. collection.
    ☐ d. resignation. _____

Add your scores for questions 1–6. Enter the total here and on the graph on page 160. **Total Score** _____

145

73 ¡Huelga!

A cry of "¡*Huelga!*—Strike!" rang out over the vineyards in 1965 as the National Farm Workers Association was finally feeling powerful enough to stop work and demand pay raises from three of the largest California grape growers. Two growers agreed to recognize the farm workers' union and increase the pay, but the nation's largest table grape producer did not agree, and the strike continued. Organizations, individuals, political leaders, and religious leaders lent their support to the union. The National Farm Workers Association organized rallies, marches, hunger strikes and asked people to not buy California grapes unless the grapes had the union label.

The leader of these workers was César Chávez (1927–1993). A teenaged Chávez had left his family's migrant life years ago to take a job pruning vines and picking grapes near Delano, California. During World War II, he served in the U.S. Navy, but after the war he began to organize Mexican-American farm workers. His intention was to improve the living and working conditions of the migrant farm workers, who, Chávez believed, would continue to remain powerless unless they had their own union.

In September 1962, he founded the National Farm Workers Association in Fresno, California, and traveled through the California grapefields trying to convince workers of the benefits of union membership. We can help you stand up to your Anglo bosses, Chávez told them, and help you get decent wages and working conditions. The union strike and the nationwide boycott finally, in 1970, convinced the largest vineyards and most other California table-grape growers to agree to the union contract, a contract that helped to improve salaries and conditions for union farm workers.

Main Idea	1			
			Answer	**Score**
		Mark the *main idea*	M	15
		Mark the statement that is *too broad*	B	5
		Mark the statement that is *too narrow*	N	5

a. Mexican-American grape pickers struck successfully for better pay and conditions. ☐ ____

b. The National Farm Workers Association is a union. ☐ ____

c. César Chávez had been a picker. ☐ ____

Score 15 points for each correct answer.   **Score**

Subject Matter   **2**   This passage is mainly about
☐ a. the life of César Chávez.
☐ b. the success of the National Farm
Workers' strike.
☐ c. the Mexican-American heritage.
☐ d. agricultural developments in the grapefields.   _____

Supporting   **3**   The National Farm Workers called for a boycott of
Details   ☐ a. wine.
☐ b. hiring migrant farm workers.
☐ c. nonunion table grapes.
☐ d. grape growers.   _____

Conclusion   **4**   The migrant workers' union was effective insofar as
☐ a. government laws were passed to improve
their wages and living conditions.
☐ b. the public decided to buy and eat grapes.
☐ c. the boycott and strike convinced grape
growers to honor a contract.
☐ d. César Chávez began pruning vines.   _____

Clarifying   **5**   The purpose of the second paragraph is to
Devices   ☐ a. give background information about the
union leader.
☐ b. explain how the union is organized.
☐ c. describe the daily life of a migrant worker.
☐ d. list important events in the union's history.   _____

Vocabulary   **6**   The word <u>strike</u> in this passage means to
in Context   ☐ a. hit.
☐ b. set on fire by rubbing.
☐ c. cross out.
☐ d. stop work.   _____

Add your scores for questions 1–6. Enter the total here   Total
and on the graph on page 160.   Score   _____

74 Phobias

Phobias are intense, unrealistic fears that are <u>disproportionate</u> to the danger of an object or situation. People who suffer from phobias avoid the situations or objects that they fear, an avoidance that usually disrupts their daily lives. The National Institute of Mental Health has reported that 5.1 to 12.5 percent of Americans have phobias. Phobias are the most common psychiatric illness among women and the second most common psychiatric illness among men over 25.

Phobias may be divided into three classes:

1. Simple phobias, such as the fear of small animals, harmless snakes, heights, darkness, or closed spaces.
2. Social phobias, such as the fear of speaking in public, eating in public, being out in public, or attending social gatherings.
3. Agoraphobia, the fear of being in situations where escape might be difficult or embarrassing or where help might not be available if one has an anxiety attack.

Agoraphobia is the most complex and debilitating of all phobias. People with agoraphobia tend to avoid crowds, movie theaters, tunnels, bridges, and public transportation. The range of avoided situations may be so great that people suffering from agoraphobia find themselves unable to leave their homes.

Phobias are treatable through either behavior therapy or medication. In behavior therapy, a trained therapist helps the patient confront the feared object or situation in a carefully planned, gradual way in order to learn to control the physical reactions of fear. With medication, which is the preferred treatment for social phobia and agoraphobia, both anxiety and panic can be controlled.

Main Idea 1		Answer	Score
Mark the *main idea*		M	15
Mark the statement that is *too broad*		B	5
Mark the statement that is *too narrow*		N	5
a. Agoraphobia is a severe phobia.		☐	_____
b. Fears can cause people problems.		☐	_____
c. Phobias are unrealistic fears that usually respond to treatment and medication.		☐	_____

Subject Matter   **2**   Another good title for this passage is
- ☐ a. Agoraphobia: A Fear of Everything.
- ☐ b. Working with a Therapist.
- ☐ c. Why People Are Afraid.
- ☐ d. Recognizing and Overcoming Irrational Fears.   _____

Supporting Details   **3**   The number of Americans with phobias is
- ☐ a. more than 15 percent.
- ☐ b. less than 5 percent.
- ☐ c. between 5.1 and 12.5 percent.
- ☐ d. 17.6 percent.   _____

Conclusion   **4**   Phobias are considered a psychiatric illness because
- ☐ a. they are complex.
- ☐ b. they are treatable only at the National Institute of Mental Health.
- ☐ c. they are an unrealistic overreaction to objects and situations.
- ☐ d. they are contagious.   _____

Clarifying Devices   **5**   The list of phobias is presented
- ☐ a. alphabetically.
- ☐ b. from least to most severe.
- ☐ c. from most to least severe.
- ☐ d. in the order of importance.   _____

Vocabulary in Context   **6**   Disproportionate means
- ☐ a. out of proportion.
- ☐ b. able to be measured.
- ☐ c. disrespectful.
- ☐ d. extremely large.   _____

Add your scores for questions 1–6. Enter the total here and on the graph on page 160.   **Total Score**   _____

75 The City on the Rise

Although many North American cities can boast of falling crime rates and balanced municipal budgets, the U.S. Department of Housing and Urban Development reports that middle-class families continue to move to the suburbs. In the 1990s, suburbs contained 75 percent more families than did cities, compared with 25 percent more in 1970. Though salvaging the North American city as a place to live may seem impossible, many experts believe that <u>rejuvenated</u> cities can alleviate problems created by the vast suburban communities and that they could become attractive places to live for many types of people.

Some theorists say that the information age is giving cities this opportunity to grow. As e-mail and the Internet eliminate commuting to a corporate headquarters, a new generation of teleworkers, Web entrepreneurs, and knowledge-based professionals will have the freedom to live where they choose. This opportunity was once seen as the death knell for cities, as it was thought that people would move away from the cities to live in small towns, mountain villages, or remote getaways. But the exact opposite may prove true. Locational freedom means people can choose to live where it is pleasant. For some, or even many, that place is the city. A city with advanced telecommunications services, proximity to universities and libraries, neighborhoods that can be navigated on foot, concert halls, museums, and restaurants that are still open at 3 A.M. will be able to compete with the sprawling suburbs. Some experts say that the demand for an intense, active, vibrant, diverse atmosphere will increase as information technology spreads. And this sort of atmosphere is exactly what healthy cities will be ready to provide.

Main Idea	1	Answer	Score
	Mark the *main idea*	M	15
	Mark the statement that is *too broad*	B	5
	Mark the statement that is *too narrow*	N	5

a. The North American city can be a nice place to live. ☐ _____

b. More families live in the suburbs than in the cities. ☐ _____

c. The information age may provide the opportunity for cities to grow. ☐ _____

Subject Matter 2 This passage is mainly concerned with
- ☐ a. why city schools are a problem to population growth.
- ☐ b. cities of the present.
- ☐ c. cities of the future.
- ☐ d. lowering city taxes.

_____

Supporting Details 3 Between the 1970s and 1990s, the number of families living in cities
- ☐ a. declined.
- ☐ b. increased.
- ☐ c. did not change.
- ☐ d. was never specifically counted.

_____

Conclusion 4 This passage leads the reader to believe that
- ☐ a. the death knell has rung for cities.
- ☐ b. restaurants will be open all night.
- ☐ c. cities will turn into sprawling suburbs.
- ☐ d. cities may experience an increase in middle-class population.

_____

Clarifying Devices 5 The information in the first paragraph of this passage is expressed through
- ☐ a. a list of facts only.
- ☐ b. an anecdote about a personal experience.
- ☐ c. a series of steps in a process.
- ☐ d. a mix of fact and opinion.

_____

Vocabulary in Context 6 In this passage, <u>rejuvenated</u> means
- ☐ a. rebuilt from scratch.
- ☐ b. made young again.
- ☐ c. made vigorous again.
- ☐ d. improved by planting trees.

_____

Add your scores for questions 1–6. Enter the total here and on the graph on page 160.   **Total Score**   _____

Answer Key: Passages 1–25

Passage 1:	1a. **N**	1b. **M**	1c. **B**	2. **d**	3. **a**	4. **b**	5. **a**	6. **d**
Passage 2:	1a. **B**	1b. **M**	1c. **N**	2. **a**	3. **c**	4. **b**	5. **d**	6. **a**
Passage 3:	1a. **N**	1b. **B**	1c. **M**	2. **a**	3. **b**	4. **b**	5. **b**	6. **c**
Passage 4:	1a. **B**	1b. **M**	1c. **N**	2. **c**	3. **a**	4. **b**	5. **b**	6. **d**
Passage 5:	1a. **M**	1b. **B**	1c. **N**	2. **c**	3. **b**	4. **b**	5. **d**	6. **a**
Passage 6:	1a. **B**	1b. **N**	1c. **M**	2. **b**	3. **c**	4. **d**	5. **a**	6. **b**
Passage 7:	1a. **M**	1b. **N**	1c. **B**	2. **b**	3. **d**	4. **b**	5. **c**	6. **c**
Passage 8:	1a. **M**	1b. **N**	1c. **B**	2. **c**	3. **d**	4. **d**	5. **a**	6. **a**
Passage 9:	1a. **B**	1b. **M**	1c. **N**	2. **c**	3. **c**	4. **b**	5. **a**	6. **d**
Passage 10:	1a. **M**	1b. **B**	1c. **N**	2. **d**	3. **b**	4. **d**	5. **a**	6. **a**
Passage 11:	1a. **N**	1b. **B**	1c. **M**	2. **a**	3. **b**	4. **d**	5. **a**	6. **b**
Passage 12:	1a. **M**	1b. **N**	1c. **B**	2. **b**	3. **a**	4. **c**	5. **d**	6. **b**
Passage 13:	1a. **M**	1b. **B**	1c. **N**	2. **b**	3. **d**	4. **d**	5. **b**	6. **c**
Passage 14:	1a. **B**	1b. **M**	1c. **N**	2. **b**	3. **c**	4. **b**	5. **d**	6. **c**
Passage 15:	1a. **B**	1b. **M**	1c. **N**	2. **a**	3. **d**	4. **b**	5. **a**	6. **a**
Passage 16:	1a. **N**	1b. **M**	1c. **B**	2. **c**	3. **b**	4. **d**	5. **d**	6. **a**
Passage 17:	1a. **N**	1b. **M**	1c. **B**	2. **d**	3. **b**	4. **d**	5. **c**	6. **a**
Passage 18:	1a. **B**	1b. **M**	1c. **N**	2. **b**	3. **b**	4. **b**	5. **c**	6. **d**
Passage 19:	1a. **B**	1b. **N**	1c. **M**	2. **d**	3. **b**	4. **c**	5. **a**	6. **c**
Passage 20:	1a. **N**	1b. **M**	1c. **B**	2. **a**	3. **c**	4. **a**	5. **b**	6. **c**
Passage 21:	1a. **B**	1b. **N**	1c. **M**	2. **b**	3. **d**	4. **b**	5. **b**	6. **c**
Passage 22:	1a. **M**	1b. **N**	1c. **B**	2. **a**	3. **c**	4. **d**	5. **c**	6. **b**
Passage 23:	1a. **B**	1b. **M**	1c. **N**	2. **a**	3. **d**	4. **a**	5. **d**	6. **c**
Passage 24:	1a. **M**	1b. **N**	1c. **B**	2. **c**	3. **a**	4. **d**	5. **c**	6. **b**
Passage 25:	1a. **B**	1b. **M**	1c. **N**	2. **d**	3. **b**	4. **b**	5. **c**	6. **a**

Answer Key: Passages 26–50

Passage 26:	1a. **M**	1b. **N**	1c. **B**	2. **c**	3. **c**	4. **c**	5. **d**	6. **a**
Passage 27:	1a. **N**	1b. **M**	1c. **B**	2. **c**	3. **c**	4. **b**	5. **a**	6. **d**
Passage 28:	1a. **B**	1b. **N**	1c. **M**	2. **c**	3. **b**	4. **d**	5. **b**	6. **d**
Passage 29:	1a. **M**	1b. **B**	1c. **N**	2. **d**	3. **a**	4. **a**	5. **d**	6. **c**
Passage 30:	1a. **B**	1b. **M**	1c. **N**	2. **b**	3. **a**	4. **c**	5. **d**	6. **a**
Passage 31:	1a. **B**	1b. **M**	1c. **N**	2. **b**	3. **b**	4. **c**	5. **a**	6. **c**
Passage 32:	1a. **B**	1b. **M**	1c. **N**	2. **a**	3. **a**	4. **a**	5. **c**	6. **b**
Passage 33:	1a. **N**	1b. **M**	1c. **B**	2. **c**	3. **a**	4. **b**	5. **b**	6. **a**
Passage 34:	1a. **B**	1b. **N**	1c. **M**	2. **b**	3. **d**	4. **b**	5. **a**	6. **c**
Passage 35:	1a. **N**	1b. **M**	1c. **B**	2. **b**	3. **d**	4. **b**	5. **b**	6. **b**
Passage 36:	1a. **M**	1b. **N**	1c. **B**	2. **c**	3. **d**	4. **b**	5. **b**	6. **a**
Passage 37:	1a. **B**	1b. **M**	1c. **N**	2. **d**	3. **b**	4. **c**	5. **a**	6. **a**
Passage 38:	1a. **M**	1b. **N**	1c. **B**	2. **d**	3. **b**	4. **a**	5. **b**	6. **b**
Passage 39:	1a. **M**	1b. **B**	1c. **N**	2. **b**	3. **d**	4. **b**	5. **c**	6. **a**
Passage 40:	1a. **N**	1b. **B**	1c. **M**	2. **c**	3. **a**	4. **d**	5. **a**	6. **b**
Passage 41:	1a. **B**	1b. **N**	1c. **M**	2. **b**	3. **c**	4. **a**	5. **c**	6. **d**
Passage 42:	1a. **M**	1b. **B**	1c. **N**	2. **a**	3. **c**	4. **c**	5. **d**	6. **b**
Passage 43:	1a. **N**	1b. **B**	1c. **M**	2. **b**	3. **d**	4. **c**	5. **c**	6. **a**
Passage 44:	1a. **N**	1b. **B**	1c. **M**	2. **b**	3. **c**	4. **b**	5. **b**	6. **d**
Passage 45:	1a. **N**	1b. **B**	1c. **M**	2. **c**	3. **a**	4. **c**	5. **b**	6. **d**
Passage 46:	1a. **B**	1b. **N**	1c. **M**	2. **c**	3. **a**	4. **d**	5. **c**	6. **c**
Passage 47:	1a. **N**	1b. **B**	1c. **M**	2. **a**	3. **d**	4. **a**	5. **b**	6. **c**
Passage 48:	1a. **M**	1b. **N**	1c. **B**	2. **b**	3. **c**	4. **b**	5. **a**	6. **b**
Passage 49:	1a. **B**	1b. **N**	1c. **M**	2. **a**	3. **b**	4. **d**	5. **c**	6. **c**
Passage 50:	1a. **M**	1b. **N**	1c. **B**	2. **c**	3. **a**	4. **b**	5. **c**	6. **d**

Answer Key: Passages 51–75

Passage 51:	1a. **M**	1b. **N**	1c. **B**	2. **d**	3. **c**	4. **a**	5. **a**	6. **b**
Passage 52:	1a. **N**	1b. **M**	1c. **B**	2. **d**	3. **b**	4. **d**	5. **b**	6. **c**
Passage 53:	1a. **M**	1b. **B**	1c. **N**	2. **c**	3. **a**	4. **c**	5. **d**	6. **b**
Passage 54:	1a. **B**	1b. **N**	1c. **M**	2. **c**	3. **d**	4. **c**	5. **a**	6. **b**
Passage 55:	1a. **N**	1b. **B**	1c. **M**	2. **d**	3. **b**	4. **b**	5. **a**	6. **d**
Passage 56:	1a. **M**	1b. **N**	1c. **B**	2. **a**	3. **a**	4. **a**	5. **c**	6. **b**
Passage 57:	1a. **M**	1b. **B**	1c. **N**	2. **c**	3. **c**	4. **b**	5. **b**	6. **c**
Passage 58:	1a. **M**	1b. **N**	1c. **B**	2. **c**	3. **d**	4. **a**	5. **a**	6. **c**
Passage 59:	1a. **M**	1b. **B**	1c. **N**	2. **b**	3. **b**	4. **d**	5. **b**	6. **a**
Passage 60:	1a. **M**	1b. **N**	1c. **B**	2. **c**	3. **b**	4. **a**	5. **d**	6. **b**
Passage 61:	1a. **N**	1b. **B**	1c. **M**	2. **b**	3. **b**	4. **d**	5. **b**	6. **a**
Passage 62:	1a. **B**	1b. **N**	1c. **M**	2. **c**	3. **b**	4. **c**	5. **a**	6. **d**
Passage 63:	1a. **M**	1b. **B**	1c. **N**	2. **b**	3. **b**	4. **b**	5. **a**	6. **c**
Passage 64:	1a. **B**	1b. **N**	1c. **M**	2. **b**	3. **a**	4. **c**	5. **a**	6. **d**
Passage 65:	1a. **N**	1b. **B**	1c. **M**	2. **d**	3. **c**	4. **b**	5. **b**	6. **a**
Passage 66:	1a. **M**	1b. **B**	1c. **N**	2. **c**	3. **c**	4. **b**	5. **d**	6. **a**
Passage 67:	1a. **B**	1b. **M**	1c. **N**	2. **d**	3. **d**	4. **a**	5. **b**	6. **b**
Passage 68:	1a. **N**	1b. **M**	1c. **B**	2. **b**	3. **a**	4. **d**	5. **c**	6. **b**
Passage 69:	1a. **N**	1b. **B**	1c. **M**	2. **d**	3. **c**	4. **a**	5. **b**	6. **c**
Passage 70:	1a. **B**	1b. **N**	1c. **M**	2. **b**	3. **c**	4. **d**	5. **c**	6. **b**
Passage 71:	1a. **M**	1b. **N**	1c. **B**	2. **c**	3. **a**	4. **d**	5. **c**	6. **b**
Passage 72:	1a. **B**	1b. **N**	1c. **M**	2. **a**	3. **b**	4. **b**	5. **d**	6. **c**
Passage 73:	1a. **M**	1b. **B**	1c. **N**	2. **b**	3. **c**	4. **c**	5. **a**	6. **d**
Passage 74:	1a. **N**	1b. **B**	1c. **M**	2. **d**	3. **c**	4. **c**	5. **b**	6. **a**
Passage 75:	1a. **B**	1b. **N**	1c. **M**	2. **c**	3. **a**	4. **d**	5. **d**	6. **c**

Diagnostic Chart: Passages 1–25

Directions: For each passage, write your answers to the left of the dotted line in the blocks for each skill category. Then correct your answers using the Answer Key on page 152. If your answer is correct, do not make any more marks in the block. If your answer is incorrect, write the letter of the correct answer to the right of the dotted line.

	Categories of Comprehension Skills								
	1 Main Idea			Subject Matter	Supporting Details	Conclusion	Clarifying Devices	Vocabulary in Context	
	Statement a	Statement b	Statement c		2	3	4	5	6
Passage 1									
Passage 2									
Passage 3									
Passage 4									
Passage 5									
Passage 6									
Passage 7									
Passage 8									
Passage 9									
Passage 10									
Passage 11									
Passage 12									
Passage 13									
Passage 14									
Passage 15									
Passage 16									
Passage 17									
Passage 18									
Passage 19									
Passage 20									
Passage 21									
Passage 22									
Passage 23									
Passage 24									
Passage 25									

Diagnostic Chart: Passages 26–50

Directions: For each passage, write your answers to the left of the dotted line in the blocks for each skill category. Then correct your answers using the Answer Key on page 153. If your answer is correct, do not make any more marks in the block. If your answer is incorrect, write the letter of the correct answer to the right of the dotted line.

	Categories of Comprehension Skills								
	1 Main Idea				2	3	4	5	6
	Statement a	Statement b	Statement c	Subject Matter	Supporting Details	Conclusion	Clarifying Devices	Vocabulary in Context	
Passage 26									
Passage 27									
Passage 28									
Passage 29									
Passage 30									
Passage 31									
Passage 32									
Passage 33									
Passage 34									
Passage 35									
Passage 36									
Passage 37									
Passage 38									
Passage 39									
Passage 40									
Passage 41									
Passage 42									
Passage 43									
Passage 44									
Passage 45									
Passage 46									
Passage 47									
Passage 48									
Passage 49									
Passage 50									

Diagnostic Chart: Passages 51–75

Directions: For each passage, write your answers to the left of the dotted line in the blocks for each skill category. Then correct your answers using the Answer Key on page 154. If your answer is correct, do not make any more marks in the block. If your answer is incorrect, write the letter of the correct answer to the right of the dotted line.

	Categories of Comprehension Skills								
	1 Main Idea				2	3	4	5	6
	Statement a	Statement b	Statement c	Subject Matter	Supporting Details	Conclusion	Clarifying Devices	Vocabulary in Context	
Passage 51									
Passage 52									
Passage 53									
Passage 54									
Passage 55									
Passage 56									
Passage 57									
Passage 58									
Passage 59									
Passage 60									
Passage 61									
Passage 62									
Passage 63									
Passage 64									
Passage 65									
Passage 66									
Passage 67									
Passage 68									
Passage 69									
Passage 70									
Passage 71									
Passage 72									
Passage 73									
Passage 74									
Passage 75									

Progress Graph: Passages 1–25

Directions: Write your Total Score for each passage in the comprehension score box under the number of the passage. Then plot your score on the graph itself by putting a small *x* on the line directly above the number of the passage, across from the score you got for that passage. As you mark your score for each passage, graph your progress by drawing a line to connect the *x*'s.

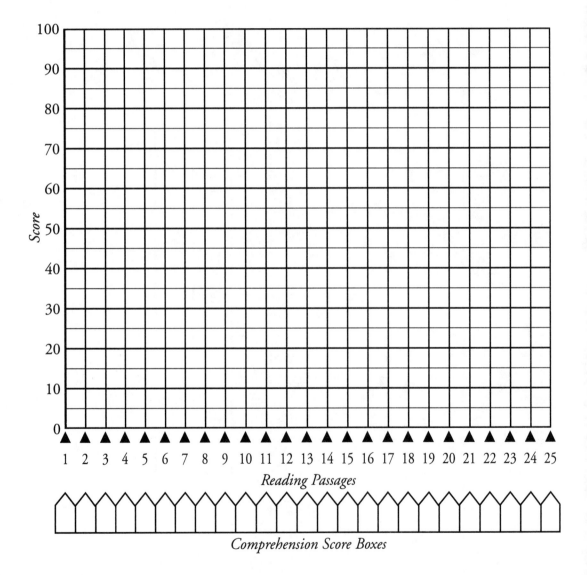

Reading Passages

Comprehension Score Boxes

Progress Graph: Passages 26–50

Directions: Write your Total Score for each passage in the comprehension score box under the number of the passage. Then plot your score on the graph itself by putting a small *x* on the line directly above the number of the passage, across from the score you got for that passage. As you mark your score for each passage, graph your progress by drawing a line to connect the *x*'s.

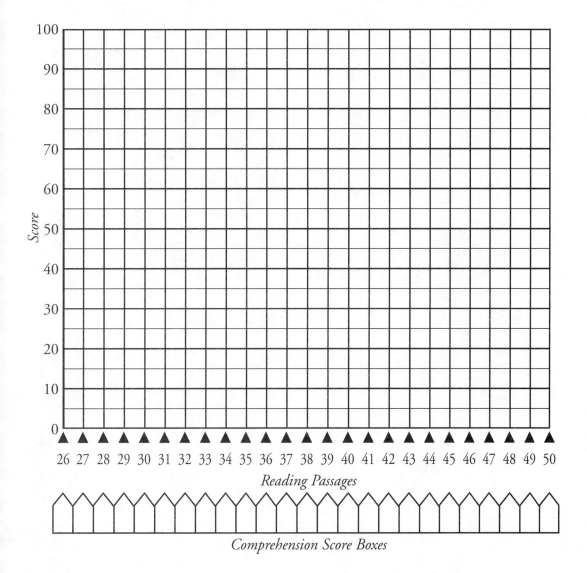

Reading Passages

Comprehension Score Boxes

Progress Graph: Passages 51–75

Directions: Write your Total Score for each passage in the comprehension score box under the number of the passage. Then plot your score on the graph itself by putting a small *x* on the line directly above the number of the passage, across from the score you got for that passage. As you mark your score for each passage, graph your progress by drawing a line to connect the *x*'s.

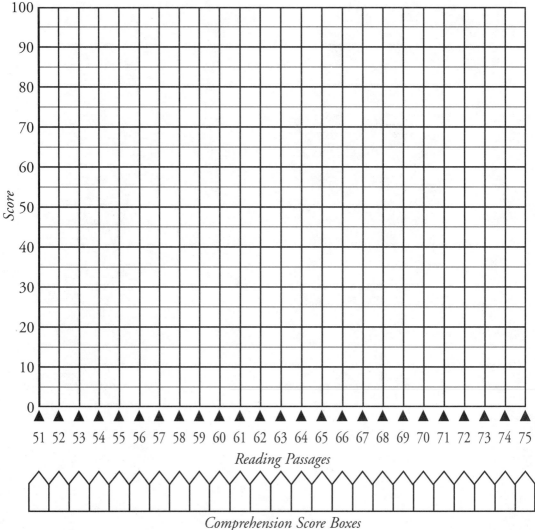

Reading Passages

Comprehension Score Boxes